CRAFTS- MEN OF QUALITY

Crafts Advisory Committee

© 1976 Crafts Advisory Committee
12 Waterloo Place
London SW1Y 4AU

ISBN 0 903798 08 5

Printed in Great Britain
by Hazell Watson and Viney, Aylesbury

Contents

How to use this book

Britain is famous for her artist craftsmen, talented men and women whose skill puts them among the best in the world. This book is an introduction to them and their work, and is specially designed for easy use as a reference book for customers and tourists. A brief introduction in Arabic, French, German and Japanese has been included for the benefit of the visitor to Britain.

The craftsmen

The selection is based on the Crafts Advisory Committee's Index of Craftsmen, all of whom have submitted their work to a panel of master craftsmen imposing the most rigorous standards. The entries are arranged alphabetically within each craft. In most cases, there is an illustration of the work. Addresses and telephone numbers are given, since craftsmen are generally willing to receive visits from intending purchasers. However, as many do not have a showroom or staff, we would ask you to respect their request to make an appointment. There is a description of the type of work done, and a biographical note, indicating where a person's work has been bought by public collections in Britain and overseas, and mentioning their most recent solo exhibitions. In some cases a bibliography is included; retail outlets are also given.

The shops

As well as selling direct, many craftsmen sell through craft shops and galleries. The addresses of these, arranged alphabetically by the name of the shop, will be found in two lists at the end of the book: shops and galleries in London, and those elsewhere.

The British Crafts Centre

The craftsmen listed in this book also display their work at the British Crafts Centre, 43 Earlham Street, London WC2 (near Covent Garden). Here there is a wide choice of craftsmen's work and a gallery offering changing exhibitions of fine craftsmanship. Also operated by the BCC is the Craft Shop V & A, at the Victoria and Albert Museum, South Kensington, London SW7.

Craftsmen Potters Shop

All potters listed as members of the Craftsmen Potters Association are entitled to sell their work at the Association's shop in Marshall Street, London W1 (parallel with, and to the west of Regent Street); most members' work is in stock.

Commissioning

All the artist craftsmen in this book will work to commission. Thus, if you would like a piece of silver or jewellery, an engraved glass, a special binding, a tapestry or a piece of furniture specially designed and made to meet your needs, you will find someone to make it for you here. Having decided what you want, and contacted the maker you have in mind, you will find him or her very helpful: you can be guided by their experience in the craft when you brief them. You should make clear how much you want to spend, agree on a delivery date and the way you will pay. If you are approaching more than one craftsman initially, then make this clear, for the quotation of each may involve a certain amount of personal commitment on his or her part.

The Crafts Advisory Committee
This body was set up in 1971 to administer the government grant to the crafts. It exists to encourage and support the crafts and makes a grant to the British Crafts Centre. At its offices at 11–12 Waterloo Place, Lower Regent Street, London sw1, the CAC runs a gallery exhibiting work by British and overseas artist craftsmen, and an information service, the Index of Craftsmen. Established craftsmen can apply for inclusion on the Index. Their work is scrutinised by a committee of master craftsmen appointed by the British Crafts Centre. If the selection committee recommends inclusion on the Index, slides of the work are generally lodged there. This library of some 6,000 colour slides is open free of charge on weekdays from 10am to 5pm, by appointment only, to the general public, and to students and teachers of crafts. To make an appointment, telephone the Index Librarian at 12 Waterloo Place (01-839 1917).

イギリスは世界でも一流の工芸家の多くいる国として有名です。この本は、それらの工芸家とその仕事の紹介であり、顧客、旅行者の参考として特に使いやすいようデザインされています。

CRAFTSMAN OF QUALITYには、イングランドとウエールズに働く 300 名以上の有能な工芸家が載つており、彼らの仕事の説明と写真、販売店と画廊のリスト等が含まれています。また、ほとんどの場合工芸家達は、前もつて連絡さえあれば、お客様の訪問を喜んで受けますので、住所や電話番号も記載されています。この本に紹介されている工芸の中には、製本、印刷と書法、ガラス吹き、ガラス彫版、金、銀細工、宝石細工、陶器、陶器彫像、織物と絵付け、木彫刻と家具造り等があります。

この本はCrafts Advisory Committee により出版され、特別に選ばれたスライドと情報の目録である工芸家の目録に基づいています。その目録は、英国一流工芸品の展示が次々と一般に公開されるウオータールー・プレース・ギャラリーに置かれています。役員はいつでも、今日の英国工芸における仕事の依頼や一般情報についてのアドバイスをいたします。

تشتهر بريطانيا بفنانيها الحرفيين الذين يعدون من بين احسن الحرفيين في العالم . ويعتبر هذا الكتاب بمثابة تعريف بهؤلاء الفنانين واعمالهم . وقد روعي في تصميمه سهولة استعماله كمرجع للعملاء والسياح .

ويشمل كتاب **كرافتسمان أوف كواليتى** قائمة باكثر من ثلاثمائة من الحرفيين الموهوبين الذين يعملون في انجلترا وويلز ،كما يشمل اوصاف وصور لاعمالهم وقائمة بالمحال وصالات العرض التي يمكن شراءها منها ، وكذلك العناوين وارقام التليفونات حيث ان هؤلاء الفنانين علي استعداد لاستقبال زائريهم من عملاء المستقبل بشرط ان يكونوا علي علم مسبق بتلك الزيارات . ومن بين الحرف اليدوية التي يتضمنها هذا الكتاب تجليد الكتب والطباعة وفن الخطوط اليدوية وتشكيل الزجاج بالنفخ والنقش علي الزجاج وحدادة الذهب والفضة وصناعة المجوهرات وفن النحت الفخاري والخزفي وطباعة وغزل المنسوجات والحفر علي الاخشاب وصناعة الاثاث .

ولقد نشر هذا الكتاب عن طريق اللجنة الاستشارية للفنون وهو يعتمد في مضمونه علي فهرس الحرفيين المقدم من اللجنة وعلي فهرس خاص بالشرائح الزجاجية والمعلومات الخاصة بالحرفيين . وقد تم ايداع الفهرس في صالة العرض في واترلو بليس حيث توجد المعارض المختلفة لاحسن الفنانين البريطانيين والمفتوحة للجمهور . ويمكن للمسئولين هناك ان يقدموا النصيحة الخاصة بالعمولات وكذلك المعلومات العامة التي تخص الفنون الحرفية المتواجدة في بريطانيا اليم .

La Grande-Bretagne est célèbre pour ses artisans d'art qui comptent parmi les meilleurs au monde. Cet ouvrage est une introduction sur eux-mêmes et sur leur travail, et il a été spécialement conçu afin que les touristes ou les clients puissent facilement le consulter, comme livre de référence.

Craftsmen of Quality comptent plus de 300 artisans de talent, exerçant leur activité en Angleterre et au Pays de Galles. Vous trouverez des descriptions et des photographies de leurs oeuvres, ainsi qu'une liste des boutiques et galeries où on peut les acquérir. Les adresses et numéros de téléphone y figurent également, car la plupart des artisans accueillent toujours avec plaisir les amateurs éventuels sous réserve qu'on les prévienne à l'avance. Dans cette édition, les différents secteurs de l'artisanat représentés sont entre autres la reliure, l'imprimerie et la calligraphie, le soufflage du verre et la gravure sur verre, l'orfèvrerie, la joaillerie, la poterie et la sculpture sur céramique, l'impression et le tissage des textiles, la sculpture sur bois et la fabrication de meubles.

Cet ouvrage est publié par le Comité consultatif de l'artisanat (Crafts Advisory Committee) et il est fondé sur leur Index des Artisans (Index of Craftsmen), répertoire spécialement choisi de diapositives et d'informations. Cet index se trouve à la Waterloo Place Gallery, où sont ouvertes au public les diverses expositions présentées par les meilleurs artisans britanniques. Le personnel pourra également vous conseiller à propos des commandes et vous donner des renseignements d'ordre général se rapportant à l'artisanat pratiqué actuellement en Grande-Bretagne.

Das britische Kunsthandwerk ist berühmt – es zählt zu den besten der Welt. Dieses Buch stellt Kunstgewerbeschaffende und ihre Arbeit vor und seine besondere Gestaltung macht es zum handlichen Nachschlagewerk für Kunden und Touristen.

Im *Craftsman of quality* sind über 300 Spezialisten des Kunsthandwerks, die in England und Wales tätig sind, aufgeführt. Neben Beschreibungen und fotografischen Abbildungen ihrer Arbeiten, enthält das Buch eine Liste der Geschäfte und Kunstgalerien, die die gefertigten Artikel zum Verkauf anbieten. Auch Anschriften und Rufnummern fehlen nicht, da Kunstgewerbeschaffende Interessenten fast immer gern begrüßen, sofern sie über deren Besuch im voraus unterrichtet sind. Dieses Buch behandelt u.a. die folgenden handwerklichen Fachgebiete: Buchbinderei, Druckereiarbeiten und Kalligraphie, Glasbläserei und -gravur, Gold- und Silberschmiedekunst, Fertigung von Schmuckstücken, Töpfer- und Keramikarbeiten, Textildruck und Webkunst, Holzschnitzerei und Möbeltischlerei.

Dieses Buch ist von dem Crafts Advisory Committee (Handwerklichen Beratungsausschuß) herausgegeben und beruht auf dessen Verzeichnis von Kunsthandwerkern, d.h. auf einem besonderen Sachregister mit Diapositiven und Informationen. Dieser Index befindet sich in der Waterloo Place Gallery, wo der breiten Öffentlichkeit in stets wechselnden Ausstellungen die besten Erzeugnisse des britischen Kunstgewerbes vorgestellt werden. Auch das Personal ist gern bereit, Auskünfte über die Vergebung von Aufträgen wie auch über das Kunsthandwerk in Großbritannien von heute zu erteilen.

BRUNSKILL Ann
The Worlds End Press, 1A Olivers Wharf,
64 Wapping High Street, London E1 LP1
tel: 01-480 6012
visitors by appointment

Limited editions of handmade books combining
craftsmanship and classical texts with modern
etchings and design. The paper is handmade and
the books are bound by hand in vellum or boxed.

Born in London. Trained, Chelsea College of
Art. CAC bursary 1975. Member of the Royal
Society of Painter Etchers. Work in Victoria &
Albert Museum; University of Liverpool;
Universities of Oxford & Cambridge;
Bibliothèque Nationale, Paris; Library of
Congress, Washington; National Library of
Australia, Canberra; Lessing J Rosenwald
collection, Alverthorpe, USA. Exhibitions:
1970, Studio Prints, London; 1972, Boadicea,
London. Publications, see articles in *Arts Review*
and *The Private Library*, 1972; *Crafts,* 16,
1975.

Sells direct to clients, also through specialist
booksellers.

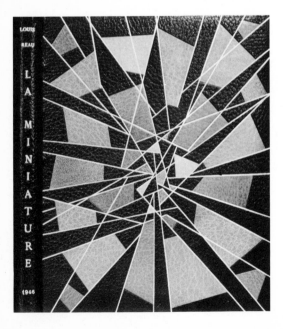

CAMPBELL Fiona
158 Lambeth Road, London SE1
tel: 01-928 1633
visitors by appointment

Fine binding usually in leather, using traditional
methods, including inlays and tooling –
combined with non-traditional design.

Born in Scotland; trained Central School of
Arts and Crafts. Member, Society of Designer-
Craftsmen; Art Workers' Guild; Designer
Bookbinders. Work in British Museum;
National Library of Scotland.

Sells direct from workshop and Scottish Craft
Centre.

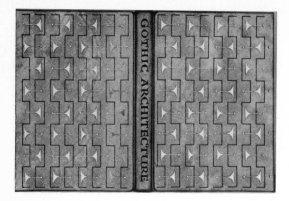

COCKERELL Sydney
Riversdale, Grantchester, Cambridge
tel: 022 021 2124
visitors by appointment

Individual tooled bindings – repair and conservation of rare books, manuscripts and documents. Marbled paper.

Fellow, Society of Antiquaries; Hon. Member, Society of Scribes and Illuminators; Fellow, National Institute of Conservation of Historic and Artistic Works; Art Workers' Guild (past Master); Double Crown Club. Work in Victoria & Albert Museum; British Museum; Liverpool Public Library; National Library of Scotland. Publications, *Marbling Paper* London 1934; 'The Binding of Manuscripts' in *The Calligrapher's Handbook* ed C M Lamb, London 1956; *The Repair of Books* London 1958; Appendix to *Bookbinding and the Care of Books* by Douglas Cockerell, London 1973; See also, *The Book Collector* Dorothy Harrop, London 1974; *Bookbinding in Great Britain*, London 1975.

Sells direct from workshop.

POWELL Roger
The Slade, Froxfield, Petersfield
Hampshire, GU32 1EB
tel: 073 084 229
visitors by appointment

Repair, conservation and rebinding of early books – decorated fine bindings for collectors – one-off commissions.

Born in London; trained, Central School of Arts & Crafts and in workshop of Douglas Cockerell & Son. Member, Double Crown Club; Art Workers' Guild. Work in collection of British Museum; Victoria & Albert Museum; Bodleian Library, Oxford; Trinity College, Dublin; Royal Irish Academy; Royal Library, Windsor; Westminster Abbey; Lichfield Cathedral.

Sells direct to clients.

RANDLE John
Whittington Court, Near Cheltenham,
Gloucestershire
home tel: 024 82 615
visitors by appointment

Limited editions of books, usually printed on
handmade paper and illustrated. Letterpress
printing from hand-set type.

Born in England. Trained, London College of
Printing. Work in Victoria & Albert Museum
Library and many other libraries in the UK.
Teaches, Malvern Hills College (short courses).

Sells direct to clients and through bookshops –
Hatchards; Bertram Rota; Maggs Bros;
Heywood Hill; John Sandoe; Libertys; Heals;
Foyles.

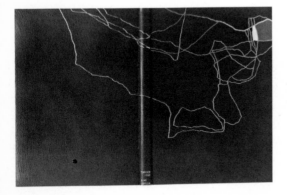

ROBINSON Ivor
Trindles, Holton, Oxfordshire, OX9 1PZ
tel: 086 77 3823

Design and execution of individual fine
bookbindings. The designs are largely linear and
restless because they derive from free
spontaneous drawings without recourse to
drawing instruments.

Born in Bournemouth. Apprenticed as a
bookbinder; further study at Bournemouth
College of Art. Silver medallist and double
bronze medallist, Prix Paul Bonet 1971. Member
of Designer-Bookbinders; Fellow, Royal
Society of Arts; Meister der Einbandkunst.
Work at British Museum; Victoria & Albert
Museum; Bodleian Library, Oxford; Hornby
Library, Liverpool; Royal Library, Stockholm;
Royal Library, Copenhagen; Röhsska Museum,
Gothenburg. Exhibitions, 1963, Hantverket
Gallery, Stockholm; 1969, Galleria del Bel
Libro, Ascona. Publications, *Introducing
Bookbinding*, 1968; many articles about work
published in Italy, Germany, Sweden,
Switzerland. See *Crafts*, 1, 1973. Teaches,
Oxford Polytechnic.

Sells direct to clients.

ROWSON Philip
Lansdowne, Weydown Road, Haslemere, Surrey
tel: 0428 3075
visitors by appointment

Speciality handmade papers for printing, stationery, calligraphy produced by traditional techniques and non-traditional techniques – free flow, translucent, inlay, fibre mix, misting, selective exposure.

Sells direct to clients.

SHANNON Faith
18 Kings Road, Kingston-upon-Thames, Surrey
tel: 01-546 0396
visitors by appointment

Presentation work and prototypes in various materials – miniature painting.

Born in India. Trained, Belfast College of Art; six months' scholarship from Belfast to Central School of Arts & Crafts and the London School of Printing; Goldsmiths' College; Royal College of Art; Scholarship from Dublin to USA. Member of Royal Ulster Academy; Designer-Bookbinders. Work in British Museum; Hornby Library, Liverpool; GAC collection. See *Crafts*, 1, 1973.

Sells direct to clients.

SMITH Philip
83 Nutfield Road, South Merstham, Redhill,
Surrey, RH1 3HD
tel: 649 2627
visitors by appointment

Binding of special books using various original
techniques – maril (patent marbled inlaid
leather); bookwalls (sets of books arranged in
panels with continuous designs linking covers of
each book – free-standing or built-in); feathered
onlay work – mainly untooled images.

Born in Lancashire. Trained, Southport School
of Art; Royal College of Art. CAC bursary
1975. Member, Society of Industrial Artists and
Designers; Designer Bookbinders; Meister der
Einbandkunst. Work in Victoria & Albert
Museum; Hornby Library, Liverpool; New
York Public Library; Museo del Oro Bogota,
Columbia. Exhibitions: 1970, Galleria del Bel
Libro, Ascona; Goldsmiths' Hall, London.
Publications, *New Directions in Bookbinding*,
London 1975; see also *Crafts*, 1, 1973.

Sells direct to clients.

BRADLEY Ray
3 Orchard Studios, Brook Green,
London W6 7BU
tel: 01-602 1840
visitors by appointment

Stained glass and allied architectural media.
Windows, walls, or screens of glass by
traditional methods, glass appliqué laminations,
slab glass, sand blasting, silvering and acid
etching. Public and private commissions for
ecclesiastical and secular buildings.

Born in Surrey. Trained, Wimbledon School of
Art; Royal College of Art. Awarded Sir Arthur
Evans Travelling Scholarship by the Glaziers
Company, 1966. Awarded CAC bursary 1976.
Fellow of the British Society of Master Glass
Painters. Work in a number of churches and
restaurants. Teaches, Reigate School of Art &
Design; Reading University.

Sells to commission direct to client.

CLARKE Dillon
86 Yoakley Road, London N16 0BB
tel: 01-800 4487
visitors by appointment

Studio glass – functional and sculptural pieces –
free-blown or mould blown.

Trained, Stoke-on-Trent College of Art;
Hornsey College of Art; Royal College of Art.
Work in Victoria & Albert Museum; Derby
Museum and Art Gallery; Leicester Museum and
Art Gallery; Kent Education Authority
collection; Museum of South Australia.
Exhibitions: 1970, Pace Gallery, London; 1971,
Salix, Windsor; 1972, Sandbach Arts
Association, Cheshire; 1973, 1974, Amalgam,
Barnes; 1975, Upper Street Gallery, London;
Pisces Designs, London. Teaches, Middlesex
Polytechnic.

Sells from workshop; Atmosphere, Samian
Galleries, Pisces, London.

DAVIS Michael
Stained Glass Studio, Digswell House,
Monks Rise, Welwyn Garden City,
Hertfordshire
tel: 043 87 5547
visitors by appointment

Work to commission in traditional (leaded,
painted and stained glass) and modern (glass/
resin appliqué) techniques. Also glass and resin
sculptures (usually boxed landscapes) and leaded
glass medallions.

Born in London. Trained, St Martin's School of
Art; Hornsey College of Art. Member of the
British Society of Master Glass Painters. Teaches,
Barnfield College of Further Education.

Sells direct to clients and Chelsea Glassworks,
London; Mariposa; The Kimpton Crafts
Centre; Seven Springs Gallery.

HONEY Roger
1 Abbot's Ride, Farnham, Surrey
tel: 025 13 3190
visitors by appointment

Glass and ceramic goblets.

For illustration see *Pottery*.

IGLEHART Edward
North Glen Studio, Palnackie, Castle Douglas,
Kirkcudbrightshire, Scotland
tel: 055 660 200
visitors by appointment

'Lampwork', works blown from clear
borosilicate tubing using oxy-fuel gas
equipment and coloured glass made in the studio
from borosilicate waste and colouring oxides.
Larger pieces frequently employ 'frames' or
'external armatures' of steel or other metals.

Studied metal working at Brooklyn Museum,
New York, USA and chemistry at University of
Florida, USA and New York University; also
worked in chemical research. Member of
American Crafts Council.

Sells direct to public and at Heals, London.

MORGAN James
11 Woodland Road, Leytonstone, London E11
tel: 01-539 6085
visitors by appointment

Decorative mirror panels in glass or plastic, hand
painted, screen printed; colour designs.

Trained at Royal College of Art. Teaches at
Chelsea School of Art, Chesterfield College of
Art, Derbyshire.

Sells to commission.

PEARCE Simon
Bennettsbridge, County Kilkenny, Ireland
tel: Kilkenny 27175
visitors by appointment

Functional glass, jugs, goblets, bowls.

Studied pottery in New Zealand with Harry Davis. Trained as glassblower at Royal College of Art; The Glass House. Awarded Coras Trachtala Design Scholarship. Worked at seven glass factories in Scandinavia. Member of Society of Designers in Ireland.

Sells direct to public and through David Mellor.

SOLVEN Pauline
Ravenshill Farmhouse, Cliffords Mesne,
Nr Newent, Gloucestershire
tel: 0531 820109
visitors by appointment

Sculptural blown glass, free and flowing shapes generally derived from nature, some serving a functional purpose.

Trained at Royal College of Art. Work in collection of London County Council; Kent County Council; Leicester County Council; Corning Glass Museum, New York; Museum of South Australia; Malmo Museum, Sweden. Exhibition: 1971, Salix Gallery, Windsor. Teaches at Isleworth Polytechnic.

Sells at The Glasshouse, London.

TOOKEY Fleur
The Glasshouse, 27 Neal Street, London WC2
tel: 01-836 9785
visitors welcome

Sculptural blown glass, some purely for visual
enjoyment, some serving a functional purpose.
Generally rather floral in inspiration, the
emphasis being on delicate form rather than on
colour; larger pieces combined with metal.

Trained at Hereford College of Art; Brighton
College of Art; Stourbridge College of Art.

Sells direct to public.

DINKEL E. Michael
The Grange, Bussage, Nr Stroud, Gloucestershire
tel: 045 388 2368
visitors by appointment

Glass engraving and pottery modelling.
Trained at Royal College of Art where he also
taught for many years. Member of Royal Society
of Painters in Water Colours. Public collections
in Dudley Art Gallery; Tate Gallery. Exhibition:
1972, Stroud Subscription Rooms.

Sells on commission to individual clients.

DINKEL Madeleine
233 King Street, Hammersmith, London w6
tel: 01-748 4891
visitors by appointment for commissions only

Engraved glass; windows and plateglass, goblets,
bowls, etc; lettering and heraldry.

For illustration see *Lettering*.

DREISER Peter
18 Rowland Avenue, Kenton, Middlesex
tel: 01-907 9251
visitors by appointment for commissioning only

Copper wheel engraving, low and high relief
work, combination of stone and diamond wheels
and points when necessary; also seal stone
engravings on rings.

Born in Cologne, trained at the Glass Technical
School for Art Glass Rheinbach (Bonn) W.
Germany. Member of Royal Miniature Society;
Society of Designer-Craftsmen; The British Art
League; The Glass Circle; The Guild of Glass
Engravers. Work in collections of Portsmouth
City Museum; the Foreign Office; London
County Hall; The Fishmongers Livery
Company. Teaches at Morley College, London.

Sells direct from workshop.

GORDON Harold
Greywalls Studio, Forres, Morayshire, IV36 0ES
tel: 030 92 2395
visitors are welcome

Engraving by means of various copper wheels
fed with abrasives; plants, animals, birds, crests,
coats of arms, monograms, fishing subjects on
crystal goblets, decanters and blocks of crystal.

Born in Forres, Scotland. Trained at Edinburgh
College of Art. Member of Guild of Glass
Engravers.

Sells direct to public and at Scottish Craft
Centre; Ell Shop.

HUTTON John

Studio Barn, Oxford Road, Clifton Hampden,
Oxfordshire, OX14 3EW
tel: 086 730 7490
visitors by appointment

Large-scale engraving on flat glass; more
concerned with the art than the craft, with a
painter's approach.

Born in New Zealand. Past Chairman, Society
of Mural Painters; Hampstead Arts Council.
Past Trustee, Arkwright Arts Trust. Member,
Guild of Glass Engravers; Art Workers Guild.
Work in collections of Victoria & Albert
Museum; Royal Scottish Museum, Edinburgh;
Bolton Museum; Corning Glass Museum, New
York; National Gallery of Wellington;
Portsmouth City Museum; Coventry
Cathedral; Guildford Cathedral; Chelmsford
Cathedral; New Zealand House; Shakespeare
Centre. Exhibitions: 1970, Ashgate Gallery,
Farnham; 1972, Octagon Theatre, Bolton.
Published *Glass Engravings of John Hutton*. See
Crafts, 16, 1975.

Sells to commission.

MOSCOVITCH Timothy

158 Trinity Street, Huddersfield,
West Yorkshire, HD1 3DX
visitors by appointment

Screenprinted mirrors, screenprinted mirrored
photograph frames and mirrored plant-pot
holders. Also etched glass tables, windows and
doors.

Trained Loughborough College of Art and
Royal College of Art. Member of the Textile
Institute and of the Society of Designer-
Craftsmen. Work in collection of Huddersfield
Education Authority. Exhibitions: 1973, White
Rose Galleries, Yorkshire; 1974, New Gallery,
College of Art, Batley, Yorkshire. Teaches, The
Polytechnic, Huddersfield.

Sells, Presents, Treasure Island, London;
Birmingham Arts Shop; Craft Harvest.

PEACE David
Abbots End, Hemingford Abbots,
Huntingdon, PE18 9AA
tel: 0480 62472
visitors by appointment

Presentation glass, lettering and heraldry,
predominantly windows.

Trained at Royal Institute of British Architects.
Member of Society of Designer-Craftsmen; Art
Workers Guild – Master. Work in collections of
Victoria & Albert Museum; Manchester City
Art Gallery; Birmingham City Museum; Royal
Scottish Museum, Edinburgh; Kettle's Yard,
Cambridge University; Corning Glass Museum,
New York, USA. Exhibitions: 1968, All
Hallows Arts Centre, London Wall; 1968, The
Minories, Colchester; 1969, Wisbech Museum;
1973, Kettle's Yard, Cambridge.

Sells to commission.

PENNELL Ronald
2 Lower Bibbletts, Hoarwithy,
Hereford & Worcester HR2 6QF
tel: 043 270 324
visitors by appointment

Gem and seal engraving, also engraving on gold
and silver.

Trained at Moseley Art School. Awarded medal
for goldsmiths and silversmiths work 1955;
Lucas prize 1958; City of London prize; stone
engraving scholarship to Germany. Fellow of
Royal Society of Arts. Work in collection of
Worshipful Company of Goldsmiths.
Exhibition: 1974, Waterloo Place, London.
Publications: *Deutsche Goldschmiedezeitung/
European Jeweller; Deutsche Graveurzeitung,
Glyptik von Ronald Pennell;* 'Gem Engraving' in
The Saturday Book; 'Gem Engraving', *Crafts*, 6,
1974.

Sells direct to public.

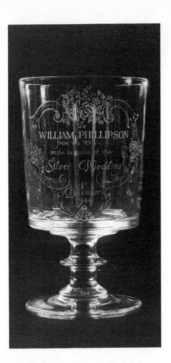

PHILLIPSON Wyn
Bourne Lodge, Boxmoor, Hertfordshire
tel: 044 27 2178
visitors by appointment

Individual pieces, lettering and heraldic design.

Trained Edinburgh College of Art. Member, Society of Designer-Craftsmen.

Sells to commission direct to client.

RICKARD Stephen
The Old Vicarage, Vicarage Park,
London SE18 7SX
tel: 01-854 3310
visitors by appointment

Glasses designed and engraved. Wheel engraving by flexible drive and abrasive wheels.

Trained at Royal Academy in sculpture where awarded gold medal. Fellow, Royal Society of British Sculptors; Fellow, Society of Designer-Craftsmen. Work in collections of Victoria & Albert Museum; Corning Glass Museum, New York.

Sells direct to public and to commission.

WEBSTER Jane
23 Peel Street, London w8 7PA
tel: 01-727 3773
visitors by appointment

Glass designed and made for special occasions, either copper-wheel or diamond-point engraved, sometimes sand blasting, cutting, mirroring or gilding included. Glass used can be blown full lead crystal, bent optical glass, or ground and polished blocks.

Trained Southern College of Art, Portsmouth; Stourbridge College of Art; awarded Princess of Wales Scholarship to Royal College of Art. Fellow, Society of Designer-Craftsmen.

Sells to commission direct to client.

WHISTLER Laurence
Little Place, Lyme Regis, Dorset, DT7 3HR
tel: Lyme Regis 2355
visitors by appointment

Engraving on blown glass, flat panels and windows.

Educated Balliol College, Oxford. Awarded CBE 1974. FRSL; President of Guild of Glass Engravers; Hon. Fellow Balliol College, Oxford. Work in collection of Victoria & Albert Museum; Fitzwilliam Museum, Cambridge; Royal Scottish Museum, Edinburgh; Brighton Art Gallery; Bristol Art Gallery; Corning Glass Museum, New York; Glenbow Museum, Calgary, Alberta. Exhibitions: 1969, Thomas Agnew's; 1971, Kettle's Yard, Cambridge; 1971, Marble Hill, Twickenham. Autobiography *The Initials in the Heart; The Engraved Glass of Laurence Whistler; Engraved Glass, 1952-1958; Pictures on Glass; Whistler Glass.*
See *Crafts*, 18, 1976.

Sells to commission direct to client.

WHISTLER Simon
5 Fullerton Road, London SW18
tel: 01-870 6083
visitors by appointment

Engraving of pictorial subjects.

Trained with his father, Laurence Whistler.
Member, Guild of Glass Engravers.

Sells to commission.

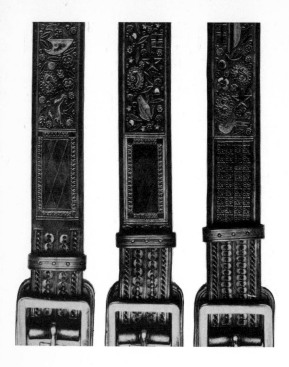

WILLIAMS John
69 London Road, Canterbury, Kent, CT2 8LW
visitors by appointment

Hand-stitched leather work, tooled and coloured
– bags, belts, folders, chessboards. On all but the
smallest stitching, the thread used is made by
hand by the traditional saddler's method. The
work is done with a variety of saddler's,
bookbinder's and general embossing tools, and is
coloured with leather dye. Also furniture
painted with oil paint.

Born in Bristol. Trained, Oxford University;
Leeds College of Art. Work in Museum of
Leathercraft; Bethnal Green Museum.
Publication, article in *Golden Hands Encyclopaedia
of Crafts*, Marshall Cavendish, 1976. Teaches
painting at Canterbury College of Art.

Sells direct to clients; Blades, London; Oxford
Gallery.

BAILEY Keith

10 Meldreth Road, Shepreth, Royston,
Hertfordshire
tel: 0763 60565
visitors by appointment

Memorial or civic lettering in all media but
mainly slate and stone. Architectural carvings
are mostly heraldic or restoration. Also produces
sculptures and designs to commission, bookplates,
etc.

Trained, Liverpool School of Art; Manchester
School of Art; worked at the Galizia Bronze
Foundry and as assistant to David Kindersley.
Member, Society of Designer-Craftsmen. Work
in churches, parks and public buildings all over
the country. Exhibition: 1967, Cambridge
Building Centre.

Sells direct to clients.

BASU Hella

During academic term:
Daytime:
Regional College of Art, Wilberforce Drive,
Hull, North Humberside
tel: 0482 224311
Evening:
4 Muirfield Park, Hull, HU5 3JF,
North Humberside
visitors by appointment

The work explores the relationship between
verbal texts and their visual presentation in terms
of lettering, style, arrangement, colour scheme
and media – usually based on poems.

Trained, Kassel Art College. Member, Society of
Designer-Craftsmen. Work in Victoria &
Albert Museum; Herbert Art Gallery &
Museum, Coventry. Exhibitions: 1975, Pan
Gallery, Goethe Institute Toronto and National
Library, Ottawa; Image Gallery, USA; Janus
Gallery; National Museum of Wales; Vaughan
College; Studio 10½; Kulturamt, Germany.
Publications, article in *Visible Language*,
Cleveland Museum of Art, 1971; article in *Arts
& Crafts in Education*, London, 1973. Teaches.
Regional College of Art, Hull.

Sells direct to clients and through Heals, London:
Oxford Gallery; Studio 10½.

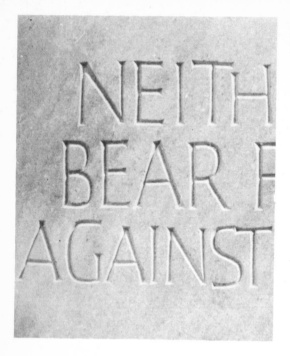

Calligraphy

is the most direct form of all artistic expression

JUST AS EACH MOVEMENT
OF THE DANCER IS ABSOLUTE
SO EVERY GESTURE
OF THE CALLIGRAPHER
IS ESSENTIAL

IT IS NOT THE MEANING OF THE
CHARACTER BUT THE WRITING –
THE MOVEMENT OF EXECUTION
AND THE ACTION ITSELF –
THAT IS IMPORTANT

BEYER Ralph
45 St. Winifreds Road, Teddington, Middlesex
tel: 01-977 4599
visitors by appointment

Lettering and letter design in all materials –
wood, metal, stone etc – also carved sculpture –
related to buildings and outdoor spaces.

Trained, Central School of Art & Design;
Chelsea School of Art; worked as assistant to
David Kindersley. Work in Victoria & Albert
Museum; Coventry Cathedral; Royal Mint;
various British Universities and churches;
University of Kentucky, Library. Teaches,
University of Reading.

Sells direct to clients.

CHILD Heather
188 Cromwell Road, London sw5 0sj
tel: 01-373 1681
visitors by appointment

Calligraphic manuscript books on vellum or
paper, poetry or prose. Framed calligraphic
works and calligraphic work for ceremonial
occasions. Heraldic designs – book plates – book
illustrations – botanical paintings.

Born in Hampshire. Trained, Chelsea School of
Art; Westminster School of Art. Fellow, Society
of Designer-Craftsmen; Member, Society of
Scribes and Illuminators. Work in Victoria &
Albert Museum; Guildhall, London; Drapers'
Company; Fishmongers' Company; Nuffield
College, Oxford; Harrond University Library,
Boston Public Library, Hunt Botanical Library,
USA. Publications, *Decorative Maps*, London,
1956; *Amorial Bearings of the Guilds of London*,
London, 1960; *Calligraphy Today*, London,
1965; *Heraldic Design*, London, 1965;
Christian Symbols, London, 1971; edited
Formal Penmanship, London, 1971.

Sells direct to clients.

CRAIGHEAD Sister Meinrad
Stanbrook Abbey, Callow End
Hereford & Worcester
visitors by appointment

Poster designs, based on Christian scriptural texts, which are relief prints painted with acrylics.

Born in Arkansas, USA. Trained, University of Wisconsin and in Vienna; went to Barcelona on a Fulbright award. Now a Benedictine nun at Stanbrook Abbey. Exhibitions: 1975, Digby Stuart College of Education, London; Gallery 27, Tonbridge; Worcester City Art Gallery; Global Village Crafts, South Petherton.

Sells Heals, London; Stanbrook Abbey Sales Shop; Chapel Galleries; Global Village Crafts.

DEWEY David
Coach House, Widford, Nr Ware
Hertfordshire SG12 8RG
tel: 027 984 2410
visitors by appointment

Carved, coloured and gilded lettering and heraldry in any variety of stone, slate, marble, granite or wood, for architectural and memorial work.

Born in India. Trained in the workshop of David Kindersley. Work commissioned by many County Councils, Local Authorities, Department of the Environment.

Sells direct to clients.

DINKEL Madeleine

233 King Street, Hammersmith, London w6
tel: 01-748 4891
visitors by appointment for commissions only

Calligraphy – scrolls, illuminated addresses, books, family trees, heraldry. Publishing – book jackets, lettering display, binding designs, historic lettering, drawn, painted and written. Ceramics – plaques and inscriptions in majolica and stoneware, inscribed presentation bowls, goblets – large outdoor architectural display lettering, plaques and numerical, in coloured glazes and stoneware. Gold and silver – lettering design for plates, bowls, goblets.

Born in London. Trained, Edinburgh College of Art; Royal College of Art. Awarded CAC Bursary 1976. Member, Society of Industrial Artists; Fellow, Society of Designer-Craftsmen; Member, Art Workers' Guild. Exhibition: 1970, All Hallows, London Wall.

Sells direct to clients.

See *Glass: engraved and etched.*

GARDNER William

Chequertree, Wittersham, Nr Tenterden
Kent, TN30 7EJ
tel: 097 77 240
visitors by appointment

Design and engraving of coinages, seals and medallic dies. Heraldry, symbolism and lettering for various media.

Trained, Royal College of Art; Central School of Arts & Crafts. Fellow, Society of Industrial Artists and Designers; Fellow, Royal Society of Arts. Commissions completed for Privy Council; House of Commons; Household Cavalry; Brigade of Footguards; Royal Marines; Home Office; Colonial Office; Post Office; London Transport; Governments of New Zealand, Guyana, Nigeria, Algeria, Cyprus, Jordan, Nepal, Ceylon, United Kingdom; Royal Society; British Medical Association; Royal Society of Arts. Exhibitions: 1963, Colorado State University, Public Library, Denver; 1965, Monotype House, London; Portsmouth College of Art.

Sells to commission direct to clients.

HECHLE Ann
23 Eastville, Claremont Road, Bath
Avon BA1 6QN
tel: 0225 61052
visitors by appointment

Manuscript books and framed pieces using calligraphy and illumination. Hangings, curtains, tablecloths, blinds, using brush lettering on material. Murals.

Born in Calcutta. Trained Central School of Arts & Crafts. Member of the Society of Scribes and Illuminators. Teaches, week and weekend courses at West Dean College.

Sells direct to clients.

KINDERSLEY David
Chesterton Tower, Chapel Street
Cambridge, CB4 1DY
tel: 0223 62170
visitors by appointment

Alphabetics and sculpture.

Trained with Eric Gill. Member of the Wynkyn de Worde Society; Society of Designer-Craftsmen; The Art Workers' Guild; Association Typographique International. Work at Victoria & Albert Museum; The Museum of Modern Art, New York; University of San Francisco; Washington University Library. Exhibitions: 1969, Folio Society, London; 1971, Curwen Gallery, London; 1972, Fermoy, King's Lynn; 1973, Vernon Gallery, Preston; 1975, Heals, London. Publications, *Optical Letter Spacing and its Mechanical Applications*, The Wynkyn de Worde Society, London, 1966; *Variations on the Theme of 26 Letters*, 1969; *Graphic Sayings*, 1971; *Graphic Sayings*, 1973 (limited Edition), published by Christopher Skelton and David Kindersley.

Sells direct to clients.

SKELTON John
Oakwood Farmhouse, Streat, Hassocks, Sussex
tel: 0273 890491
visitors by appointment

Lettering in all media – murals – small sculpture
for the home and architectural sculpture –
silverwork and beaten copper work –
headstones and memorials.

Trained, Coventry School of Art; Coventry
School of Architecture; in apprenticeship with
Eric Gill. Member of the Royal Society of
British Sculptors. Work in Chichester City
Museum; Derbyshire County Art Collection
Shakespeare Trust; Brighton City Art Gallery.
Exhibitions: 1963, Chichester City Museum;
1965, Herbert Art Gallery; 1966, University of
Sussex; 1970, Plymouth City Art Gallery; 1971,
Van der Straeten, New York; 1972, Watergate
Galleries, Washington. Teaches, West Dean
College.

Sells direct to clients.

URWICK Alison
41 Northumberland Place, London w2
tel: 01-229 8357
visitors by appointment

Calligraphy, paintings, wallhangings,
manuscript books, family trees (including
heraldry), presentation scrolls, calligraphy and
drawings for reproduction. Lettering on paper,
silk, vellum using watercolour, gouache,
Chinese ink, gold leaf and powder.

Born in Berkshire. Trained, Byam Shaw
School of Drawing and Painting. Member of the
Society of Scribes and Illuminators. Exhibition:
1975/6, Fine Arts Museum, Malta. Work in
Fine Arts Museum, Malta.

APPLEBY Malcolm
Crathes Station, Banchory,
Kincardineshire, Scotland
tel: 033 044 642
visitors by appointment

Engraving on iron, steel, alloys or precious
metals – gun decorating and one-off pieces.

Trained at Central School of Art; Royal College
of Art; apprenticed to John Wilkes, gunsmiths
of Beak Street.

Sells direct and at Collingwood, London.

ASQUITH Brian
Turret House, Youlgrave, Derbyshire
tel: 062 986204
visitors by appointment

Domestic and ceremonial silver.

Trained Royal College of Art. Fellow, Society
of Industrial Artists and Designers. Work in
collections of Worshipful Company of
Goldsmiths; Salford University; Fitzwilliam
College, Cambridge; Sheffield Corporation.
Exhibitions: 1968, Craft Centre, London; 1969,
New York; 1970, Tokyo; 1974, St Michael's
Gallery, Derby Cathedral; 1975, Silver in
Derbyshire, Youlgrave.

Sells direct and through Heals, Cameo Corner,
London; Parrots.

BENNEY Gerald
Beenham House, Beenham, Berkshire, RG7 5LJ
tel: 073 527 370
visitors by appointment

Functional and decorative objects in gold and silver.

Born Hull, trained at Brighton College of Art, under Dunstan Pruden, ecclesiastical silversmith; Royal College of Art as Royal Scholar. Liveryman of the Worshipful Company of Goldsmiths; member of Royal Designers for Industry; Fellow, Royal Society of Arts. Exhibitions: 1968, Rutland Gallery; 1973, Goldsmiths Hall. Visiting Professor of Silver and Jewellery at the Royal College of Art.

Sells to commission.

BONEHILL Richard
6–9 Benjamin Street, London EC1M 5SQ
tel: 01-253 3141
visitors by appointment

One-off pieces of jewellery and silverware to commission. Particularly interested in design of trophies and medals for special events and competitions.

Born in London. Trained, Hornsey College of Art. Licenciate Member of the Society of Industrial Artists and Designers. Exhibition: 1972, The Phoenix Theatre, Leicester, with Lynne Bradshaw.

Sells direct to clients.

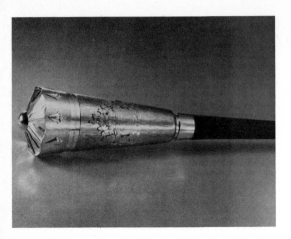

CLEN-MURPHY Desmond
Foxhole Farm, Battle, Sussex
tel: 042 462053
visitors by appointment

One-off commissions in silver, jewellery based
on architectural forms often using large natural
crystals.

Born in London, trained at Brighton Art
School. Fellow of Society of Designer-
Craftsmen. Work in the collection of
Goldsmiths' Company. Teaches at Brighton
Polytechnic.

Sells to commission.

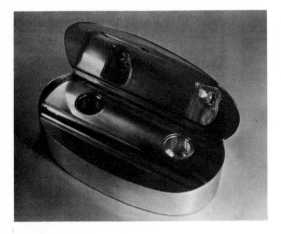

DURBIN Leslie
62 Rochester Place, London NW1 9JX
tel: 01-485 5192
visitors by appointment

Domestic, church and ceremonial silver –
medallic and coin decoration.

Awarded MVO. Member, Art Workers' Guild;
Society of Designer-Craftsmen. Work in
Collection of Gloucester Cathedral; New
College Chapel, Oxford; West London
Synagogue; Coventry Cathedral; Guards'
Chapel, Wellington Barracks. Teaches at Royal
College of Art.

Sells to commission.

ELSON Anthony
Blunt & Wray (Anthony Elson Ltd)
29 Clerkenwell Road, London EC1
tel: 01-253 0681
visitors by appointment

Domestic and ceremonial silver.

Trained Brighton College of Art; Royal College of Art – awarded silver medal. Work in collections of Sussex University; Worshipful Company of Goldsmiths; Stock Exchange.

Sells at Garrards; Hennell; Asprey; John Donald, London; Dembo; Tarratt.

FLOCKINGER Gerda
c/o Crafts Advisory Committee
12 Waterloo Place, London SW1Y 4AU
visitors by appointment

Rings, bracelets, necklaces, chains and brooches in gold and silver and both combined, using precious stones of many kinds, also cultured and natural pearls.

Born in Austria. Trained, St Martin's School of Art; Central School of Art & Design. Work in collection of Worshipful Company of Goldsmiths; Victoria and Albert Museum; City Art Gallery, Bristol; Royal Scottish Museum, Edinburgh; The Schmuckmuseum, Pforzheim. Exhibitions: 1968, British Crafts Centre; 1971, Victoria and Albert Museum, City Art Gallery, Bristol.

Sells direct to clients.

GRENVILLE John
14 Guildhall Street, Bury St. Edmunds, Suffolk
tel: 0284 4884
visitors by appointment

Church plate, domestic silver, mostly one-off
pieces to commission.

Trained School of Art Farnham and
Kingston-on-Thames; Central School of Arts &
Crafts. Work in collections of Worshipful
Company of Goldsmiths; Victoria & Albert
Museum; University of Essex; London
University. Exhibition: 1971, Ickworth House,
Bury St. Edmunds, Suffolk. Teaches Ipswich
School of Art.

Sells direct and at Cameo Corner, London;
Oxford Gallery.

HARRISON Paul
23a Victoria Road, Deal, Kent, CT14 7AS
tel: 03045 3460
visitors by appointment

Domestic, ecclesiastical and ceremonial silver.

Teaches in Art Department of Nonnington
College of Physical Education.

Sells direct and at The Tableware Centre,
London.

HAWKSLEY Anthony
Tredorwin, Nancledra, Penzance, Cornwall
tel: 073670 6964
visitors by appointment

Domestic, church, ceremonial silver –
jewellery with silver and semi-precious stones.

Trained Maidstone College of Art; Royal
College of Art. Member of Society of
Designer-Craftsmen. Work in collections of
Oxford Colleges; Victoria & Albert Museum.

Sells direct and at Payne & Son.

JACKSON Robert
6 Wickenby Drive, Sale, Cheshire
visitors by appointment

Domestic silverware, often one-off pieces.

Trained Sheffield Polytechnic; Royal College of
Art. Exhibition: 1975, Peterloo Gallery,
Manchester.

Sells direct and to commission.

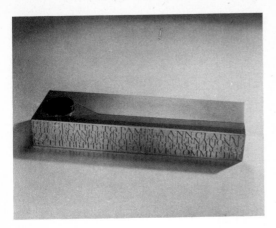

LAWS Tony
8 Garrick Street, Covent Garden,
London WC2E 9BH
tel: 01-836 7291
visitors by appointment

Range of jewellery and silverware, some large
projects, including graphics, shop design, glass
and cosmetic bottles and packaging.

Trained Gravesend School of Art; Canterbury
College of Art; Royal College of Art. Member,
Society of Designer-Craftsmen; Society of
Industrial Artists and Designers; Art Workers'
Guild. Exhibition: 1974, Portland, Oregon,
USA. Work commissioned for Coventry
Cathedral; Sussex University; Melbourne
University. Teaches, Middlesex Polytechnic.

Sells direct to public.

LESSONS Kenneth
6 Vigo Street, London W1
tel: 01-437 5531
visitors by appointment

Modern jewellery, silver and gold limited
editions and private commissions.

Trained Royal College of Art. Member,
Society of Industrial Artists and Designers.
Work in collection of Worshipful Company of
Goldsmiths. Teaches Royal College of Art.

Sells direct to public.

MARSDEN Robert
23 Collegiate Crescent, Sheffield 10
South Yorkshire
tel: 0742 661697
visitors by appointment

Individual pieces of silver or bronze, imaginary or semi-natural forms.

Born Birkenhead, trained at Royal College of Art. Teaches, Sheffield School of Art.

Sells at Electrum Gallery; Liberty, London.

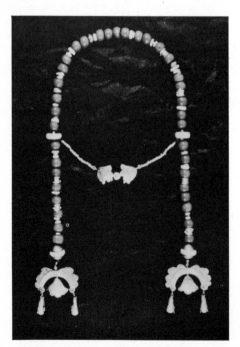

MINA Jacqueline
5 Pope's Grove, Twickenham
Middlesex, TW2 5TA
tel: 01-898 6747
visitors by appointment

Jewellery of fanciful and capricious inspiration executed in 18ct gold, often incorporating gemstones.

Trained Hornsey College of Art; Royal College of Art. Member Design & Research Centre for the Gold, Silver & Jewellery Industries; Society of Designer-Craftsmen; National Society for Art Education. Exhibitions: 1973, Ashgate Gallery; 1973, Park Square Gallery; 1975, Waterloo Place, London.

Work sold at Booty Jewellery and Argenta Gallery, London; Oxford Gallery.

MORRIS Philip

43 Endymion Road, Hatfield, Hertfordshire
tel: 30 63138*
visitors by appointment

Domestic and ecclesiastical silverware,
presentation pieces and costume jewellery –
raised hollow-ware and repoussé work.

Trained in Birmingham. Member of Society of
Designer-Craftsmen. Teaches at Cavendish
School, Hemel Hempstead.

Sells to commission.

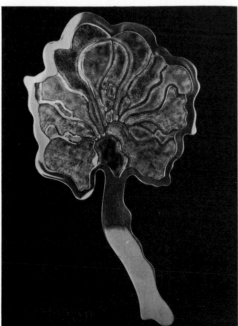

OVER Celia

Studio 211, Edgware Road, London w2
tel: 01-262 7346
visitors by appointment

Range of gold and silver objects and jewellery,
some pieces etched and/or enamelled.

Trained Royal College of Art. Member Society
of Industrial Artists and Designers. Teaches High
Wycombe College of Art and Technology.

Sells at Amalgam; Halcyon Days, London;
Oxford Gallery; Bristol Guild of Applied Art.

PAGE Peter
No. 4 The Square, Ramsbury, Nr Marlborough
Wiltshire
tel: 06722 428
visitors by appointment

One-off pieces in 18ct gold with or without
precious or semi-precious stones.

Trained Leeds Art College; Birmingham Art
College. Member, Society of Industrial Artists
and Designers; Design & Research Centre for
the Gold, Silver & Jewellery Industries.
Exhibitions: 1972, Ashgate Gallery; 1973 and
1974, Galerie Marlborough-Godard, Montreal;
1974, Ashgate Gallery, Farnham; 1974, Visual
Arts Centre, Montreal. Teaches at Birmingham
College of Art.

Sells direct and at Country Crafts.

PHIPPS William
74 Clerkenwell Road, London EC1
visitors by appointment

Domestic silverware, including cutlery,
particularly spoons; egg shaped boxes; goblets.

Trained in apprenticeship. Member, Art
Workers' Guild.

Sells to commission and Cameo Corner, London.

QUAMBUSCH Lutz
21150 Flavigny, par Les Laumes,
Grand Rue, France
visitors by appointment

Silver jewellery, sculptural objects, rings for two, three and four fingers.

Born in Berlin, apprenticed to a goldsmith in Zurich, Switzerland. Member Maison des Métiers d'Art français. Exhibitions: 1970, 1971 and 1974, Galerie M. Stute, Zurich; 1975, Goethe Institute, Stockholm; 1975, Gallery Dimitri Verscio, Tessin, Switzerland.

Sells direct from workshop.

REDFERN Keith
1 Akehurst Street, London SW15
tel: 01-788 0398
visitors by appointment

Domestic, church and ceremonial silverware, precious and semi-precious jewellery.

Member, Society of Industrial Artists and Designers. Work in collections of Worshipful Company of Goldsmiths; Universities of Essex, Sussex, Cambridge; Grand Metropolitan Hotels; Chamber of Shipping. Teaches Middlesex Polytechnic.

Sells to commission.

RODGER Ian
57 Marsh House Road, Sheffield s11 9sq
South Yorkshire
tel: 0742 364466
visitors by appointment

Traditional or experimental work in gold, silver, stainless steel, plastics.

Trained Royal College of Art. Member Society of Industrial Artists and Designers. Teaches Sheffield Polytechnic.

Sells to commission.

ROWE Michael
401½ Workshops,
401½ Wandsworth Road, London sw8
tel: 01-622 7261/2
visitors by appointment

Mostly one-off pieces in bronze, copper and silver, creating a series of containers.

Brought up in High Wycombe, trained at Royal College of Art. Member of Society of Designer-Craftsmen; Society of Industrial Artists and Designers. Work in collection of Crafts Advisory Committee. Teaches at High Wycombe College of Art.

Sells direct to commission.

THOMAS David

46 Old Church Street, Chelsea,
London SW3 5BY
tel: 01-352 8671
visitors by appointment

Jewellery in gold and silver – organic textures,
precious stones and natural crystals.

Trained Twickenham Art School; Royal
Society of Arts bursary awarded. Studied in Italy
and France, and worked in Sweden with W. A.
Bolin and Sveen Aen Gillgeon. Work in
collection of Worshipful Company of
Goldsmiths; De Beers. Exhibitions: 1965,
Detroit; 1966, Florida; 1967, St. Louis, USA;
1969, Sydney. Teaches Central School of Art &
Design.

Sells direct to public.

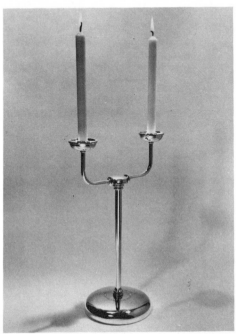

TYSSEN Keith

157 Tullibardine Road, Sheffield S11 7GP
South Yorkshire
tel: 0742 661190
visitors by appointment

Individual commissioned silverwork and
ceremonial jewellery and small batch production
of domestic pieces and jewellery.

Born Yorkshire, trained Royal College of Art.
Fellow, Society of Designer-Craftsmen;
Freeman, Worshipful Company of Goldsmiths.
Exhibitions: 1974, Aldringham Craft Market;
1975, Burnley. Teaches at School of Art and
Design, Sheffield Polytechnic.

Sells at Cob Lane Craft Shop.

WELCH Robert
The Mill, Chipping Campden, Gloucestershire
tel: 0386 840522
visitors by appointment

Silver and product design, domestic and
presentation articles.

Trained, Royal College of Art. Member
Society of Industrial Artists and Designers.
Work in collections of Museum of Applied Art,
Copenhagen; Museum of Modern Art, New
York; Museum of Applied Art, Bergen.
Exhibitions: 1967, Heals; 1967, Copenhagen;
1969, Leeds Art Gallery. Published with Alan
Crawford *Design in a Cotswold Workshop*.

Sells direct to public.

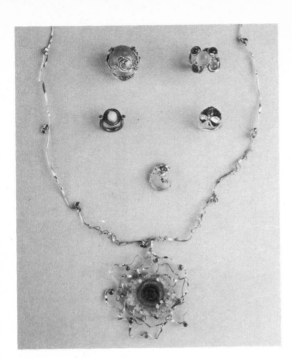

ABERDARE Sarah

1 St Peter's Square, London w6 9AE
tel: 01-748 1403
visitors by appointment

Cast jewellery in 18ct gold or silver – mainly cabochon stones, some with diamonds.

Born in London. Trained, part time at Sir John Cass College. Exhibition: 1973, Ashgate Gallery, Farnham.

Sells direct to clients and Parrots, London.

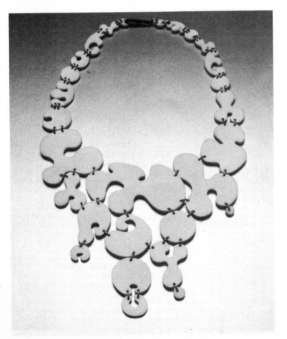

BINNS Jackie

Hillside Cottage, Horton Corner, Small Dole, Nr Henfield, Sussex
tel: 0903 814470
visitors by appointment

Jewellery and precious objects mainly in 18ct gold, ivory and enamel.

Born in Sheffield. Trained, Epsom College of Art; Kingston College of Art; Central School of Art & Design; Royal College of Art; Research Fellowship at Royal College of Art, 1968/69. Teaches at London College of Fashion.

Sells direct to clients.

See *Embroidery*.

BRADSHAW Lynne
Flat 1, 222 Westbourne Park Road, London w8
visitors by appointment

Individual pieces in silver and gold.

Born in London. Trained, Leicester College of
Art; Hornsey College of Art. Licenciate, Society
of Industrial Artists and Designers. Exhibition:
1972, Phoenix Theatre, Leicester, with Richard
Bonehill.

Sells direct to clients.

BRATMAN Ingeborg
33 New Hey Road, Huddersfield,
West Yorkshire
tel: 0484 25776
London tel: 01-499 4572
visitors by appointment

Jewellery, mainly in 18ct gold with textures,
some cast pieces – stones used include diamonds,
emeralds and pearls also small table ornaments in
18ct gold and precious stones or silver.

Trained, Hornsey College of Art; Sir John Cass
College. Licenciate, Society of Industrial Artists
and Designers. Exhibitions: 1969, Los Angeles;
1970, Craft Gallery, Knightsbridge; 1972,
Ashgate Gallery, Farnham; 1974, Ashgate
Gallery, travelling exhibition arranged by
Design and Research Centre, Cameo Corner,
Design Centre. Teaches at Sutton College of
Liberal Arts.

Sells direct to clients; Garrards; Dunhill, London.

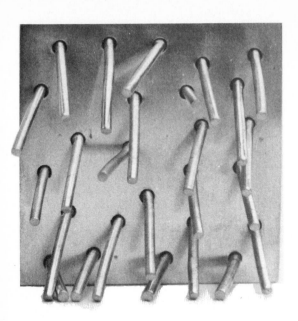

BROADHEAD Caroline

5 Dryden Street, London WC2
tel: 01-240 2430
visitors by appointment

Necklaces, bracelets, rings and brooches in ivory and silver.

Born in Leeds. Trained, Central School of Art & Design. De Beers Diamond International Award, 1974.

Sells direct to clients; Electrum Gallery, London; Oxford Gallery; Arnolfini.

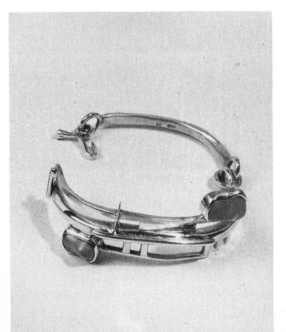

BURROWS Christopher and Pamela

c/o Crafts Advisory Committee
12 Waterloo Place, London SW1Y 4AU

Individual pieces, mainly in 9ct gold – particularly rings and pendants – with precious and semi-precious stones.

Born in England. Exhibitions: 1971, Nicholas Treadwell Gallery, London; 1972, Nicholas Treadwell Gallery; 1973, Oxford Gallery; Ashgate Gallery, Farnham.

Sell at Craftwork; Oxford Gallery.

COOKE Clarissa and Clive
53A Granville Park, Lewisham
London SE13 7DW
tel: 01-318 0115
visitors by appointment

Mostly silver – sometimes with gold decoration
– using semi-precious stones and natural
materials such as ivory, tortoiseshell and
abalone – repoussé, chasing, engraving.

Trained, Hornsey College of Art (Clarissa); Sir
John Cass College (Clive). Members of Design &
Research Centre for the Gold, Silver &
Jewellery Industries; Society of Designer-
Craftsmen. Exhibition: 1975, Booty Jewellery,
London.

Sell direct to clients; Booty Jewellery and
Argenta Gallery, London; Craftwork; Salix.

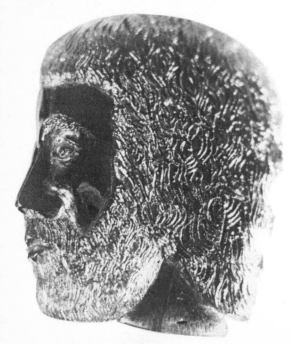

CRAXFORD Alan
14 Rusham Road, Clapham, London SW12
tel: 01-673 3770
visitors by appointment

Silver and enamel, some stones – usually in rings
– and ivory. Gold jewellery to commission.

Trained, Canterbury College of Art; part-time
at Sir John Cass College and Central School of
Art & Design. Teaches at Sir John Cass College.

Sells direct to clients; Atmosphere and Casson
Gallery, London.

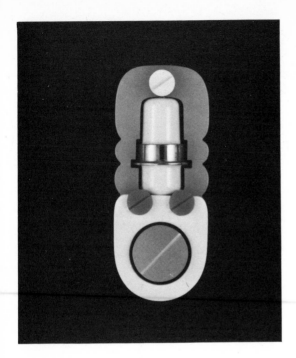

DEGEN Pierre
9 St Andrew's Road, Enfield, Middlesex
tel: 01-363 0394
visitors by appointment

Jewellery and small decorative objects –
abstract designs in many different synthetic
materials and metals.

Born in Switzerland. Trained, Ecole d'Arts
Appliqués, Switzerland. Awarded scholarship,
Bourse Fédérale des Arts Appliqués, Berne, 1972;
Diamonds International Award, 1973. Work in
Royal Scottish Museum, Edinburgh. Teaches at
Middlesex Polytechnic.

Sells direct to clients.

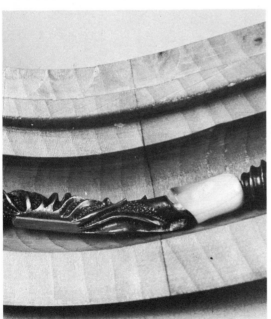

de SYLLAS Charlotte
6 Squallham's Yard, Wickmere, Norfolk
visitors by appointment

Jewellery and objects, often including carved
stones, usually contained in a carved wooden box
– commissions only.

Born in Barbados. Trained, Goldsmiths College,
School of Art; Hornsey College of Art.
Awarded CAC bursary 1976. Work in collection
of Worshipful Company of Goldsmiths;
Crafts Advisory Committee. Teaches at Royal
College of Art.

Sells direct to clients.

DICK Lexi
27 Old Street, London EC1
tel: 01-253 3693
visitors by appointment

Figurative, detailed jewellery in a variety of
materials, including gold, silver, carved and
inlaid steel, wood, ivory and glass.

Born in London. Trained, Ravensbourne
College of Art; Royal College of Art.
Worshipful Company of Gold and Silver
Wyre Drawers Award, 1974; Travel
Scholarship, 1974; Anstruther Award, 1975;
Goldsmiths Award, 1975.

Sells direct to clients.

DONALD John
120 Cheapside, London EC2
tel: 01-606 2675
visitors by appointment

Jewellery in 18ct gold.

Born in Surrey. Trained, Farnham School of
Art; Royal College of Art. Fellow of Society of
Industrial Artists and Designers. Numerous
exhibitions held throughout the world.

Sells direct to clients.

EDWARDS Rod
31 Highgate High Street, London N6
tel: 01-348 9811
visitors by appointment

Sculpture and jewellery trophies in 18ct, 22ct or
pure gold and silver using gemstones of every
type, and natural materials such as wood,
minerals and alabaster.

Born in Australia. Member of Design &
Research Centre for the Gold, Silver &
Jewellery Industries. Work in collection of
Worshipful Company of Goldsmiths.
Exhibition: 1969, Bonython Gallery, Sydney.
Teaches at Camden Institute.

Sells direct to clients.

GREER Rita
44 Wallisdean Avenue, Baffins Pond,
Portsmouth, Hampshire PO3 6HA
tel: 0705 20308
visitors by appointment

Figurative jewellery, especially for children, and
small boxes in silver and painted enamels – doll's
house artifacts such as cutlery.

Born in West Country. Trained, Portsmouth
College of Art; Royal College of Art.
Exhibition: 1974, Oxford Gallery. Publications,
An introduction to Art and Craft, London, 1974.

Sells direct to clients and through Oxford
Gallery.

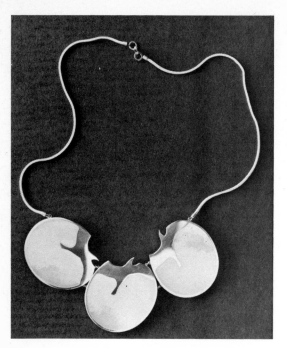

HERON Susanna
c/o Electrum Gallery, 21 South Molton Street
London WIY IDD
tel: 01-629 6325
visitors by appointment

Silver with 'pliqué à jour' resin inlay – main
concerns: colour, varying translucencies,
reflectivity and wearability.

Born in Welwyn Garden City. Trained,
Falmouth School of Art; Central School of Art
& Design. Work in collection of Worshipful
Company of Goldsmiths; Stedelijk Museum,
Amsterdam; Royal Scottish Museum,
Edinburgh; National Museum of Wales,
Cardiff; Crafts Advisory Committee
collection. Exhibitions: 1972, Electrum
Gallery London; 1974, Electrum Gallery,
Arnolfini Bristol.

Sells direct to clients; Electrum Gallery, London;
Arnolfini.

H-J KAFIRI Fotini
Unit 5, World's End Passage, World's End,
King's Road, London SW5
visitors by appointment

Jewellery and objects in different colours of gold
and silver – also uses natural materials such as
ivory, jet, ebony and rock crystal.

Born in Greece. Trained, Hornsey College of
Art; Royal College of Art. Awarded
scholarship by the National Organisation of
Hellenic Handicrafts, 1969-72; Licenciate of
Society of Designer-Craftsmen; Licenciate of
Society of Industrial Artists and Designers.
Teaches at West Surrey College of Art and
Design.

Sells direct to clients.

HUBBLE Brian
3 Arlington Cottages, Sutton Lane, London w4
tel: 01-995 9780
visitors by appointment

Small jewellery, mostly in silver.

Trained, Central School of Art & Design.
Member of Royal Institute of British Architects.
Teaches at Thames Polytechnic.

Sells direct to clients.

JAMES Duncan
49 Banbury Road, Brackley
Northamptonshire NN13 6BA
tel: 028 03 2948
visitors by appointment

Gold and silver jewellery, commemorative
pieces, trophies.

Born in Oxfordshire.

Sells direct to clients and through Asset gallery
London; Oxford gallery; Salix.

JENKINS Cynthia
27 Old Street, London EC1V 9HL
tel: 01-253 3693
visitors by appointment

Gold and coloured stone jewellery – some diamond and silver jewellery.

Born in Cambridge. Trained, Royal Academy School of Painting. Goldsmiths, Silversmiths, and Jewellers Arts Council First Prize, 1973. Member, Art Workers Guild. Teaches at Barking College of Technology; The Stanhope Institute.

Sells direct to clients; Booty Jewellery and Cameo Corner, London.

LEVITT Felicity
45 Longfield Avenue, Mill Hill, London NW7 2EH
tel: 01-203 2605
visitors by appointment

Jewellery incorporating sculptural and natural forms.

Born in London, trained Hornsey College of Art.

Sells direct to clients.

McGLUE Kevin
41 Slaithwaite Road, London SE13
tel: 01-852 5204
visitors by appointment

Silver rings inlaid with coloured resin in
cloisonné style.

Work sold to commission and at The Great
Frog London; Cob Lane Craft Shop;
Craftwork.

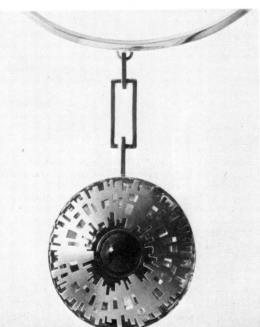

MAER Stephen
18 Yerbury Road, London N19 4RJ
tel: 01-272 9074
visitors by appointment

Individual pieces and small editions of jewellery
in silver and gold, incorporating precious and
semi-precious stones, mostly constructed and not
cast.

Born in London, trained Royal College of Art
and in industry. Member, Society of
Designer-Craftsmen; Design & Research
Centre for the Gold, Silver & Jewellery
Industries. Exhibition: 1973, Ashgate Gallery,
Farnham. Teaches Central School of Art &
Design; Sutton College of Liberal Arts.

Sells direct and at Casson Gallery and Cameo
Corner, London.

MANHEIM Julia
15 High London, 121 Hornsey Lane, London N6
tel: 01-272 9415
visitors by appointment

Carved ebony and silver, sometimes mother of pearl.

Born London, trained Hornsey College of Art: Central School of Art & Design.

Sells at Electrum Gallery London; Oxford Gallery; Arnolfini.

MANNHEIM Catherine
23 Glebe Place, London SW3
tel: 01-352 2342
visitors by appointment

Mainly figurative subjects in silver and gold – also uses ivory, tortoiseshell, stones and titanium.

Born in South Africa. Trained, Central School of Art & Design; Werkkunstschule, Düsseldorf. Work in Crafts Advisory Committee collection. Teaches at Richmond Adult Education College.

Sells direct to clients and Electrum Gallery, London; Arnolfini.

MICHAELSON Susan
101 Constantine Road, London NW3
tel: 01-485 3516
visitors by appointment

Jewellery made from fine silver wire, stones and coloured silks.

Trained, Hornsey College of Art. Publication, *Jewellery*, London 1975. Teaches at East Ham College of Technology.

Sells direct to clients.

MURRAY Clare
Shephards Bakery, Station Road, Tydd Gote, Wisbech, Cambridge
tel: 094 576 242
visitors by appointment

Mice, flowers, birds, trains, villages, trees with apples – rings, bracelets, necklaces, in brass, silver, gold, copper and titanium with other materials such as ivory, ostrich egg-shell, coral, coconutshell, applewood and boxwood.

Born in Buckinghamshire. Exhibitions: 1973, Craftwork, Guildford; 1974, Booty.

Sells direct to clients and through Booty and Casson Gallery, London; Craftwork.

NEVARD Carol
52 Middle Lane, Crouch End, Hornsey
London N8
tel: 01-348 0727
visitors by appointment

Mainly individual pieces in silver – gold to
commission.

Trained, Walthamstow College of Art;
Birmingham College of Art; Hornsey College
of Art.

Sells direct to clients and through Cameo
Corner, London.

PACKARD Gilian
Workshop: Bourn House
Sapiston Road, Honington
Bury St Edmonds, Suffolk, IP31 1RJ
tel: 035 96 606
London Office:
8-2 Sterling Court
3 Marshall Street, London W1V 1LQ
tel: 01-437 5902
visitors by appointment

Jewellery in gold and some silver – often set with
stones.

Born in Newcastle. Trained Kingston-upon-
Thames School of Art; Royal College of Art.
Member of Society of Designer-Craftsmen;
Design & Research Centre for the Gold, Silver
& Jewellery Industries; Freeman of the
Worshipful Company of Goldsmiths. Work in
collection of Worshipful Company of
Goldsmiths. Teaches at Central School of Art &
Design.

Sells direct to clients.

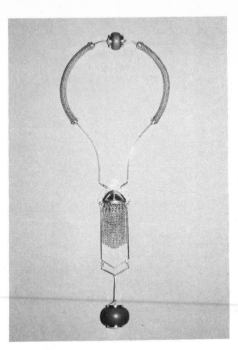

PINDER Michael
16 The Cloisters, Windsor Castle, Windsor
Berkshire SL4 1NJ
tel: 95 66523
visitors by appointment

Individual pieces, usually silver, often
incorporating rosewood, palisander, ebony,
ivory, amber, resin or porcelain.

Born in Windsor. Trained, Manchester
Polytechnic. Rentokil Trust Fund Scholarship to
Copenhagen, 1973/74. Member of Society of
Designer-Craftsmen; Midland Group of
Artists. Teaches at Isleworth Polytechnic.

Sells direct to clients.

POSTON David
Middle Farm House, Rotten Row,
Theddlethorpe, Mablethorpe,
Lincolnshire LN12 1NX
tel: 052 13 3257
visitors by appointment

Individual pieces in a wide range of principally
natural materials including bone, stone, ivory,
hemp, woods, tortoiseshell, cotton, leather and
steel made from a primarily tactile viewpoint.

Born in Moscow. Trained, Bournemouth
College of Art; Hornsey College of Art.
Exhibitions: 1975, Arnolfini Bristol, Electrum
London. See *Crafts 9*, 1974.

Sells direct to clients; Electrum, Casson Gallery,
London; Folkcrafts; Arnolfini.

RAMSHAW Wendy
c/o Crafts Advisory Committee,
12 Waterloo Place, London SW1Y 4AU

Silver and 18ct gold, one-off pieces, lathe-turned shapes using enamels, multi-coloured semi-precious stones.

Born in Sunderland. Trained, Newcastle College of Art; Reading University. In 1970, De Beers prizewinner; 1972, Council of Industrial Design Award; 1974, Johnson-Mathey Award for Platinum Jewellery Design; CAC Bursary; 1975, De Beers Diamond International Award. Fellow, Society of Industrial Artists and Designers; Freeman of the Worshipful Company of Goldsmiths. Work in the National Museum of Wales, Cardiff; Philadelphia Museum of Art; Stedelijk Museum, Amsterdam; Worshipful Company of Goldsmiths. Exhibitions: 1970, 1971, Oxford Gallery; 1972, Electrum Gallery, London; Park Square Gallery, Leeds; 1973, Goldsmiths Hall; 1974, Sunderland Art Gallery; Scopas, Henley.

Sells direct to clients; Electrum, London; Oxford Gallery.

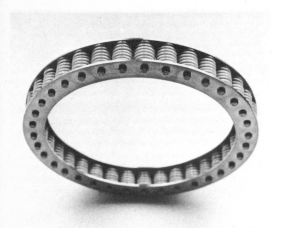

SPILLER Eric
9 Hillhead Terrace, Aberdeen
visitors by appointment

Jewellery and small objects in precious and non-precious materials – geometrical forms.

Born in Staffordshire. Trained, Central School of Art & Design; Royal College of Art. Work in Goldsmiths Hall.

Sells direct to clients; Booty Jewellery, Electrum, London.

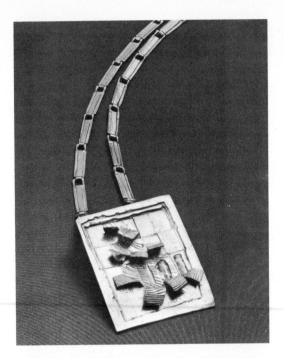

STIEGER Jacqueline
Welton Garth, Welton, Nr Brough,
East Yorkshire
tel: 0482 668323
visitors by appointment

Mainly gold jewellery, sculpture in wood, stone,
bronze and precious metal – specialises in casting
gold and bronze.

Trained, Edinburgh College of Art. Royal
Scottish Academy Award, 1957. Work in
collections of Church Rudolphstetten, Zurich;
St. Margaret's, Glasgow; Worshipful Company
of Goldsmiths. Exhibitions: 1972, Galerie
Riehentor, Basel; 1974, Galerie Riehentor;
1975, Park Square Gallery, Leeds.

Sells direct to clients.

TREEN Gunilla
c/o Crafts Advisory Committee,
12 Waterloo Place, London SW1Y 4AU

Combination of several types of material, often
plastics, together with metals and semi-precious
stones, sometimes with mobile parts inside –
recent work shows more emphasis towards use
of silver and gold, with continuing use of semi-
precious stones and ivory.

Born in Nottingham. Trained, Birmingham
College of Art and Design; Central School of
Art & Crafts. Awarded Design Research
Fellowship, Worshipful Company of
Goldsmiths, 1971 – 1973. Work in the Stedelijk
Museum, Amsterdam; Royal Scottish Museum,
Edinburgh. Teaches at Morley College.

Sells direct to clients and Electrum, London;
Arnolfini.

TURNER Anne
c/o Crafts Advisory Committee,
12 Waterloo Place, London SW1Y 4AU

Individually designed jewellery with emphasis on sculptural qualities rather than decoration.

Born in Lincolnshire. Trained, High Wycombe College of Art. Licenciate of the Society of Designer-Craftsmen.

Sells direct to clients.

WATKINS David
c/o Crafts Advisory Committee,
12 Waterloo Place, London SW1Y 4AU

Neck ornaments and bracelets in acrylic and gold or silver – one-off pieces and limited editions.

Born in Wolverhampton. Trained, Reading University. Awarded 1st Prize, De Beers Diamonds Today, 1974. Work in The Science Museum, London; Bristol City Art Gallery; Abbot Hall Museum, Kendal; Goldsmiths Hall; CAC collection. Exhibitions: 1973, Goldsmiths Hall; 1974, Arnolfini, Bristol; Waterloo Place Gallery, London; Scopas, Henley.

Sells direct to clients and at Arnolfini.

WERGE-HARTLEY Jeanne
5 Maisemore Gardens, Emsworth,
Hampshire PO10 7JU
tel: 02434 3586
visitors by appointment

Jewellery in silver and 18ct gold, cut and uncut
stones, transparent enamels – also small-scale
silversmithing, specialising in the use of
hardenable silver.

Born in Leeds. Trained, Leeds College of Art.
Fellow, Society of Designer-Craftsmen;
Member of the Design & Research Centre for
the Gold, Silver & Jewellery Industries. Teaches
at Portsmouth College of Art and Design.

Sells direct to clients; Bohun Gallery; Design
Mine.

WHITBY Emily
1 Castle Street, Totnes, South Devon
tel: 080 46 3542
visitors by appointment

Jewellery in silver and uncut stones – individual
pieces.

Trained, Chelsea School of Art; Central School
of Art & Design. Member of Devon Guild of
Craftsmen.

Sells direct to clients.

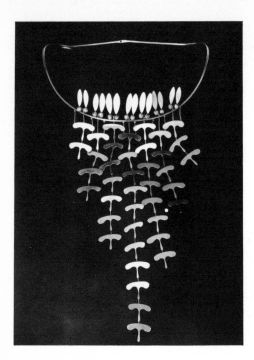

ZAHN Helga
8 Upper Park Road, London NW3
tel: 01-722 9887
visitors by appointment

Jewellery in gold and silver, precious and semi-precious stones, natural uncut stones, found objects, plastic, glass and enamels.

Born in Germany. Trained, Central School of Art & Crafts; Leeds College of Art. Awarded Gold Medal – Internazionale Handwerksmesse, Munich, 1966; CAC Bursary, 1975. Work in collection of National Museum of Wales, Cardiff; Worshipful Company of Goldsmiths; Schmuckmuseum, Pforzheim. Exhibitions: 1974, National Museum of Wales, Cardiff; 1976, Waterloo Place Gallery, London. Teaches at Middlesex Polytechnic.

Sells direct to clients.

BOUVERIE Bertrand
Blue Ridge House, Halstead, Essex
tel: 078 74 2165
visitors by appointment

Animal modelling in 'ciment fondu' finished with a surface coating of metal.

Born in London. Trained Byam Shaw School, Notting Hill. Exhibitions: 1962, Minories, Colchester; 1968, Theatre Royal, Bury-St-Edmunds; 1971, Gainsborough House, Sudbury.

Sells direct and to commission.

JONES Irene
The Cottage, West Collaton, Poundstock, Bude, Cornwall
tel: 028 885 209
visitors by appointment

Pebbles painted with figures or landscapes in gouache.

Born at Beeston, Nottinghamshire. Trained at Nottingham College of Arts and Crafts.

Sells direct and at Troika.

SMITH Ivan
Woodside, Sneads Green, Nr Droitwich,
Hereford & Worcester WR9 0PY
tel: 029 923 650
visitors by appointment

Glassmakers' tools. Wrought steel objects.

Born in Herefordshire. Trained at
Loughborough College. Consultant for wrought
iron-work with the Council for Small Industries
in Rural Areas.

Sells direct to commission.

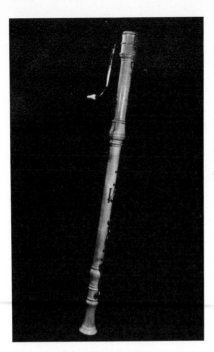

DOLMETSCH Carl
Arnold Dolmetsch Ltd, King's Road,
Haslemere, Surrey
tel: 0428 51432/3
visitors by appointment

Recorders, harpsichords, virginals, spinets,
clavichords, viols, lutes, Celtic harps, etc.

Born in France. Trained under Arnold
Dolmetsch. Awarded CBE. Hon. Doctorate of
Letters of Exeter University. Member, The
Dolmetsch Foundation; The Art Workers'
Guild; Incorporated Society of Musicians; The
Society of Recorder Players; Viola da Gamba
Society; Lute Society; Galpin Society. Published
various books on playing the recorder and on
the interpretation of early music.

Sells direct to clients.

GARROD Donald
274 Rotten Park Road, Birmingham 16,
West Midlands
tel: 021 429 4668 or 01-935 6948
visitors by appointment

Harpsichords and virginals in traditional styles
and materials.

Awarded MBE. Member, Craftsmen Potters
Association. 1973 Work featured on T.V.
Nationwide Programme. Publication, 'Making
Single Manual Harpsichord' in six parts in
Woodworker 1975. Teaches Selly Oaks Colleges,
Birmingham.

Sells to commission.

GOBLE Robert
Greatstones, Kiln Lane, Headington,
Oxford OX3 8HQ
tel: 0865 61685
visitors by appointment

Harpsichords, spinets and clavichords made to
own design or copied from traditional
instruments.

Sells direct to clients.

GOTTLIEB Stephen
27 Old Street, London EC1
tel: 01-253 3693
visitors by appointment

Lutes, tenor and bass instruments, and wire-
strung chitarroni.

Born England. Trained as architect. Member
Galpin Society; Lute Society. Teaches London
College of Furniture.

Sells direct; also at Spanish Guitar Centre.

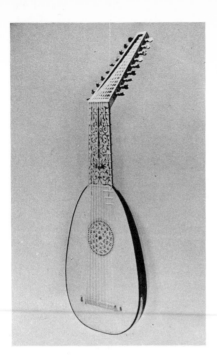

HEALE Michael
14 Market Street, Guildford, Surrey
tel: 0483 63096
visitors by appointment

Viola da Gamba, some keyboard instruments, based upon antique instruments.

Apprenticed to Arnold Dolmetsch of Haslemere; Journeyman with Martin Sassmann of Germany. Work in collections of Miami University, USA; Glasgow University; Kansas State University, USA.

Sells direct.

McCURDY Alec
Woodland Leaves, Cold Ash, Nr Newbury, Berkshire
tel: 0635 63258
visitors welcome

Cellos.

Studied with Stanley Davies of Windermere; Edward Barnsley of Froxfield. Exhibition: 1975, Imperial Tobacco Cello Festival at Colston Hall, Bristol. 1976 Featured in CAC sponsored film 'Making a Cello' by Roger Hill.

Sells direct to commission.

MORLEY John
Robert Morley & Co Ltd, 4 Belmont Hill,
Lewisham, London SE13
tel: 01-852 6151
visiting 9 – 5 pm Monday to Saturday

Clavichords, Spinets, Virginals, Harpsichords
and Harps based on original instruments of 17th
and 18th century designed to accommodate
changes of temperatures and humidities
associated with central heating and overseas
climate by the use of modern materials including
adhesives.

Born London. Trained Northern Polytechnic
London; Meisterschule fur Orgel & Klavierbau
Ludwigsberg; Workshop training, J. G. Morley.
Awarded Evelyn Broadwood Scholarship;
Silver Medal Milan Trienalle. Past President
Piano Manufacturers Association; Institute of
Musical Instrument Technology; Member Early
Musical Instrument Makers Association; Galpin
Society.

Sells direct to commission and Morley Galleries,
London.

PAUL John
Parkway, Waldron, Heathfield, Sussex TN21 0RH
tel: 043 52 2525
visitors by appointment

Making and restoration of harpsichords,
clavichords and early pianos.

Exhibition: 1956, Towner Art Gallery,
Eastbourne.

Sells to commission.

WOOLLEY Dennis
Stock Farm House, Churt, Farnham, Surrey
tel: 042 873 6206
visitors by appointment

Harpsichords, spinets, virginals and clavichords
based on or copied from classical instruments.

Trained, in engineering at Wandsworth
Technical College; in music at Trinity College
of Music. Member, Galpin Society; Institute of
Musical Instrument Technology.

Sells direct to clients.

ABDALLA Mohammed
13 King Henry's Road, London NW3
tel: 01-722 8260
visitors by appointment, at weekends

Decorative and functional pots, stoneware;
individual pieces and commissions.

Trained Khartoum College of Art; Central
School of Arts and Crafts; Post-graduate
diploma, North Staffordshire College of
Technology. Teaches, Camden Arts Centre.

Sells direct from workshop.

ASENBRYL Oldrich
Pottery and Studio, Rhiw Awel,
Bryncroes-Sarn, Pwllheli, Gwynedd.
tel: 075 883 381
visitors welcome

Reduced stoneware pottery, ceramic sculpture,
tiles, experimental work, architectural
commissions.

Trained art college, Czechoslovakia. Exhibitions:
1968, Prague; 1971, Chalfont St Giles; 1972,
Wardour School Gallery; 1975, Ceramic
Symposium, Gatlinburg, Tenn. USA. See
E. Lewenstein and E. Cooper, *New Ceramics*.

Sells direct from workshop and at Heals,
London; Scopas.

ASTBURY Paul
28A Percy Road, Shepherd's Bush,
London W12 9QA
no visitors

Ceramic sculpture in stoneware and porcelain.

Born in England. Studied Stoke-on-Trent
College of Art; Royal College of Art. Work in
Inner London Education Authority Collection;
Liberty & Co., London. One-man show touring
Belfast, Cork, Limerick, Dublin, 1975. See
Studio International, Sept. 1974; *Art & Artists*,
Dec. 1974; *Art & Antiques*, Dec. 1974; *Arts
Review*, Dec. 1974; *Collecting Antiques*, Jan. 1975;
Crafts, Jan. 1975. Teaches Middlesex
Polytechnic.

Sells direct from workshop.

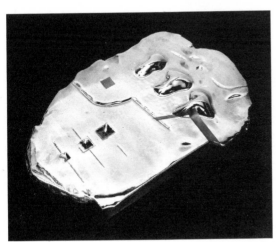

BALDWIN Gordon
1 Willowbrook, Eton, Windsor, Berkshire
tel: 95 65064
visitors by appointment

Individual pieces in stoneware, earthenware and
porcelain, slabbed, coiled, cast, thrown, press
moulded. Work is sculptural, also often with
function, generally in small series of variations
on a theme.

Born in England. Trained Central School of
Arts and Design. Fellow, Society of Designer-
Craftsmen. Work in London, GLC Collection;
Victoria & Albert Museum; Kendal, Abbotts
Hall Gallery; Leicester Education Authority;
Paisley, City Museum. Exhibitions: 1970,
Oxford Gallery; Covent Garden Gallery; 1973,
Windsor, Salix. See reviews in *Crafts*, 4, 6, 9, 10,
11 and *Ceramic Review*, 22, 28, 29, 30. Teaches
Central School of Art & Design and Eton
College, Windsor.

Sells direct from workshop and at Casson
Gallery, London; Oxford Gallery; Salix.

BARRETT-DANES Alan
The Laurels, 83 Chapel Road, Abergavenny,
Gwent, Wales
tel: 0873 4329
no visitors

White earthenware, hand modelled and press
moulded, lustre glazed, individual pieces are
worked around one main theme – frogs,
mushrooms, cabbages.

Born London. Trained Maidstone College of
Art; Stoke-on-Trent College of Art; North
Staffs College of Technology. Member of the
Society of Industrial Artists and Designers. Work
commissioned by Warwickshire County
Council; Welsh Arts Council; Buckingham
County Council; Stoke-on-Trent, City
Museum. Exhibitions: 1968, Arts Council; 1969,
Keele University; 1970, Heal's, London, Bristol
Guild; 1973, Weighton Gallery, York. See
Ceramic Review, 36 and John Dickerson, *Pottery
Making*, London 1974. Teaches, Cardiff College
of Art.

Sells direct from workshop and Oxford Gallery.

BARRON Paul
The Pottery, Thornfield, Bentley, Farnham,
Surrey
tel 025 13 2209
visitors at weekends by appointment

Largely reduced stoneware (gas fired). Pieces are
one-off and in short series. All are wheel made.
Glazes are an important feature.

Born in Berkshire. Trained Royal College of
Art. Member, Craftsmen Potters Association;
Society of Designer Craftsmen. Work in
Victoria & Albert Museum, Loans Collection;
National Gallery of Victoria, Melbourne;
Städtisches Museum, Osnabrück; Narodni
Museum, Prague. Exhibitions: 1970, Tokyo;
1973, Guildford. Articles in *Ceramic Review*, 20,
21, 24 and *Pottery Quarterly*, 1973. Teaches West
Surrey College of Art, Farnham.

Sells direct from workshop; Craftwork.

BARRY Val
86 Cecile Park, London N8 9AU
tel: 01-340 3007
visitors by appointment

Individual pieces, stoneware and porcelain, thrown and slab built, with wax-resist decoration.

Born Yorkshire. Trained Sir John Cass School of Art, London. Member, Craftsmen Potters Association. Gold Medal, 1975, International Ceramics Competition, Faenza, Italy. Exhibition: 1971, Gallery 273, London.

Sells direct from workshop and at Atmosphere; Casson Gallery; Boadicea, London; Salix; Peter Dingley; Bluecoat Centre.

BARTON Glenys
72 Brocklebank Road, London SW18
tel: 01-874 0015
visitors by appointment for commissions only

Precision ground bone china sculpture, individual pieces and small editions.

Born Stoke-on-Trent. Trained Royal College of Art. British Prizewinner, International Ceramics Exhibition, Victoria & Albert Museum, 1972. Working for one year under the patronage of J. Wedgwood, 1976. Work in Victoria & Albert Museum; Royal Scottish Museum, Edinburgh; Leeds Museum and Art Gallery; Reading Museum and Art Gallery; Portsmouth Museum and Art Gallery; Southampton Museum and Art Gallery; Moderna Museet, Stockholm. Mural 200 ft square on exterior wall of Kensington Hilton Hotel, London. One-man shows: 1973, Museum of Decorative Arts, Copenhagen; Oxford Gallery; 1974, Angela Flowers Gallery. Article in *Ceramic Review*, 34. Visiting lecturer Royal College of Art.

Sells from workshop; Angela Flowers, London; Oxford Gallery.

BIRKS Tony
Manor Farm, Caundle Marsh, Sherborne,
Dorset DT9 5LX
tel: 096323 448
visitors by appointment

Mainly stoneware, glazed sculpture and
functional objects, mostly slab built.

Born in Manchester. Studied Slade School of
Art; Oxford University; Central School of Art
& Crafts. Award winner, Westward Television
Award for Ceramics, 1973. Publications: *The
Art of the Modern Potter*, 1967; *The Potter's
Companion*, 1974; *Outline Guide to Pottery*, 1975;
See *Ceramic Review*, 36, 1975.

Sells direct from workshop and at Amalgam,
London; Salcombe Art Club Gallery.

BENNETT Anthony
17 The Broadway, Ore, Hastings, East Sussex
tel: 0424 434 645
visitors by appointment

Cast earthenware, coil built or press moulded
pieces, human or animal forms, generally with
exaggerated proportions to emphasise particular
attitudes or qualities. Moulds are used not for
mass production but to make several variants of
one piece.

Born in Worcestershire. Trained Stourbridge
College of Art, Wolverhampton Polytechnic
and Royal College of Art. Teaches full time,
Hastings College of Further Education.

Sells direct from workshop and from Treadwell
Gallery, London.

BELL-HUGHES Beverley and Terry
Garden Workshop, Potterscroft,
Oakshade Road, Oxshott, Surrey
tel: 970 2485
visitors by appointment

Individual pieces in stoneware fired to 1280°C
and handbuilt porcelain pieces, with white
barium glaze. Also make earthenware and
slipware.

Trained Sutton College of Liberal Arts and
Harrow School of Art. Members, Craftsmen
Potters Association. Exhibition: 1971, Heal's.

Sell direct from workshop and from Boadicea
and Twenty-first Century, London.

BLACKMAN Audrey
Wood Croft, Foxcombe Lane, Boars Hill,
Oxford
tel: 0865 735148
visitors by appointment

Figurines in porcelain or stoneware

Trained Goldsmiths' College; Reading
University; Oxford Technical College. Fellow,
Society of Designer-Craftsmen; Craftsmen
Potters Association; Society of Women Artists.
Porcelain ballet groups for Pennsylvania Ballet
Company, Philadelphia. Work in Fitzwilliam
Museum, Cambridge; Hanley Museum,
Stoke-on-Trent; Paisley Museum; Cecil Higgins
Museum, Bedford; Melbourne University
Collection; Magdalen College Collection,
Oxford.

Sells direct from workshop.

BLANDINO Betty
New House, St Hilary, Nr Cowbridge,
South Glamorgan CF7 7DP, South Wales
tel: 044 63 3998
visitors by appointment

Thin-walled hand-built individual pots and
bowls ranging from pinch pots to larger pots,
decorated with oxide washes and natural
stoneware glazes.

Born London. Trained Goldsmiths College.
1973, awarded prize by Welsh Arts Council.
Work in collections of Welsh Arts Council;
University College Cardiff; National Museum
of Wales, Cardiff; Towner Art Gallery; Trinity
College, Camarthen. Exhibition in association
with 20th Century Festival of Music, New Hall,
University College, Cardiff; 1975
Commonwealth Art Gallery.

Sells direct and at Heals, London; Artisan.

BRIGHT Kenneth
31 Granville Park, Lewisham, London SE13
tel: 01-852 9244
visitors by appointment

Ceramic sculptures fired at stoneware
temperatures with ash glazes thinly applied.

Trained Portsmouth College of Art and
Goldsmiths College. Work in Durham
University Collection; Dudley College;
Portsmouth Civic Gallery; Isle of Wight
County Hall. Exhibitions: 1971, Ferro,
Wolverhampton; 1973, Liverpool. Teaches,
Goldsmiths College.

Sells from workshop.

BRITTON Alison
74 Brondesbury Road, London NW6
tel: 01-328 4245 (home) and 01-387 6230
(workshop)
visitors by appointment

Hand-painted earthenware tiles and other semi-functional objects.

Born Harrow, Middlesex. Trained Central School and Royal College of Art. See *Ideal Home*, October 1975; *Vogue*, October 1975. Teaches Paddington Institute and Portsmouth Polytechnic.

Sells direct from workshop and Casson Gallery, and Strangeways, London; Quadrangle; Ashgate Gallery.

BROCK Hilary
44 High Street, Husbands Bosworth,
Leicestershire
tel: 085 882 362
visitors by appointment

Figures and groups with a strong Edwardian and early twentieth-century flavour, in ash-glazed stoneware, part thrown, part modelled, using printing techniques (from his training as an illustrator) for surface texture.

Born in Barry, Wales. Trained Cardiff College of Art. Exhibitions: 1972, Belgrade Theatre, Coventry; 1973, Peter Dingley Gallery, Stratford on Avon. Teaches at St Paul's College of Education, Stretton.

Sells in Heals, London; Newsons of Enfield; Collection; Studio 10½; Bluecoat Display Centre; Focus; Peter Dingley.

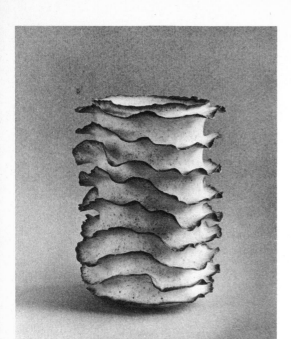

BURNETT Deirdre
Kiln Yard Cottage, 48 Gipsy Hill, London SE19
tel: 01-670 6565
visitors by appointment only

Individual pieces in oxidised stoneware or
porcelain, thrown and pinched, or pinched
alone.

Born in Simla, India. Trained St Martin's
School of Art. Member of Craftsmen Potters
Association. Work in Museum of Modern Art
Collection, New York. Exhibitions: 1975, Peter
Dingley Gallery, Stratford on Avon; Amalgam,
London; Gallery 359, Nottingham; Craftwork,
Guildford. See *Ceramic Review*, 29, 1974; *Design
Magazine*, March 1975; *Arts Review*, May/June
1975; *Brides*, September 1975. Teaches at
Wimbledon School of Art.

Sells direct from workshop and Amalgam,
Atmosphere, Best of British, Boadicea and
Casson Gallery, London; Forum; Primavera;
Craftwork; Bluecoat Display Centre; Gallery
359; Oxford Gallery; Peter Dingley.

BURR Graham
7 Egerton Drive, Greenwich, London SE10
tel: 01-692 2634
visitors by appointment
Ceramic sculpture, press moulded, with white
matt glazes, painted.

Born in Essex. Trained Chelmsford School of
Art and Camberwell School of Art. Member of
Craftsmen Potters Association. Work in
Hertfordshire Education Committee Collection;
GLC Collection, London; Bradford City Art
Gallery; Norwich Castle Museum. Exhibition:
1975, British Crafts Centre, London. See
Ceramic Review, 32, 34, 1975. Teaches at
Ravensbourne College of Art.

Sells direct from workshop.

CAIGER-SMITH Alan

Aldermaston Pottery, Aldermaston RG7 4LW, Berkshire
tel: 073 521 3359
visitors by appointment

Thrown, built or press moulded domestic and decorative earthenware, usually covered in opaque white tin glaze, brush painted in colours or with smoked lustre brush work. Most of the work is wood fired.

Born in Buenos Aires. Trained Central School of Art & Design and Camberwell School of Art. Member Craftsmen Potters Association; Society of Designer-Craftsmen. Work in Victoria & Albert Museum; National Gallery of Victoria, New South Wales; Canberra, Australian National University; Paisley Museum; Reading Museum. Exhibitions: 1970, Peter Dingley, Stratford on Avon; 1971, London, British Crafts Centre; Sturt Workshops, Mittagong, New South Wales; 1972, Wessex Design Workshops, Winchester; 1973, Craftsmen Potters Association; 1974, Craft Centre, South Yarra, Melbourne; 1975, Salix, Windsor. Published *Tin-glaze Pottery in Europe and the Islamic World*, Faber, 1973. See E. Lucie Smith, *The World of the Makers*.

Sells from pottery and Primavera; Oxford Gallery; Salix.

CARDEW Michael

Wenford Bridge Pottery, St Breward, Bodmin, Cornwall
tel: 020 885 471
visitors by appointment

Functional pottery, stoneware.

Born in Wimbledon. Studied Exeter College, Oxford; workshop training, The Leach Pottery, St Ives. Set up potteries at Vumé Dugamé and Abuja (Ghana) in West Africa, where he spent twenty years. Has run Wenford Bridge Pottery since 1939. Awarded Silver Medal, first prize for Thrown Pottery, by Worshipful Company of Turners. Member, Craftsmen Potters Association. Work in collection of Victoria & Albert Museum; Bristol Museum; Cheltenham Art Gallery; Hanley Museum, Stoke-on-Trent; Minneapolis Institute of Art; Montreal Museum of Fine Art. Recent exhibitions: 1975, Craftsmen Potters Association; 1976, Boymans-van Beuningen Museum, Rotterdam. Published *Pioneer Pottery*, 1969. See John Houston and others, *Michael Cardew*, 1976. Films on Michael Cardew: *Abuja Pottery* and *Mud and Water Man* were made by Alister Hallum, 1971 and 1973.

Sells direct from workshop.

CASSON Michael
Pottery Workshop, High Street, Prestwood,
Nr Gt Missenden, Buckinghamshire
tel: 024 06 2134
*visitors by arrangement; workshop open for sales
every Saturday*

Thrown domestic stoneware and porcelain,
individual pieces and short series.

Trained Harrow School of Art. Member,
Craftsmen Potters Association. Exhibitions:
1972, British Crafts Centre; 1973, Craftsmen
Potters Association; 1975, Craftwork, Guildford
and Casson Gallery, London. Numerous articles
in *Pottery Quarterly, Ceramic Review; Pottery in
Britain Today*, Tiranti, 1967. A film, *Michael
Casson, Studio Potter* was made by Cirus Films in
1964.

Sells direct from workshop; from Casson
Gallery, London; Craftwork; Peter Dingley.

CHERNOV Nancy
Finca la Follenca, Apdo 137, Estapona, Malaga,
Spain
visitors welcome at any time

Individual pieces – Raku tea-bowls; tableware
and flower pots for Bonzai trees.

Trained University of California and Royal
College of Art. See John Dickerson, *Raku, a
handbook*, London 1972. Teaches at Estepona,
Malaga.

Sells in workshop and Treadwell, London; Salix.

CHILDS Adrian
Ffestiniog Pottery, Blaenau Ffestiniog,
Gwynedd, Wales
visitors by arrangement

Sculptures and murals with kinetic elements and
a range of once-fired domestic earthenware.

Trained at Hornsey College of Art. Work in
Southampton Art Gallery and Portsmouth Art
Gallery.

Sells direct from workshop.

CLARK Kenneth
10A Dryden Street, London WC2
tel: 01-836 1660
visitors by arrangement

Earthenware tiles and architectural ceramics for
private houses, hotels and board rooms, using
brushwork and coloured glazes. These are
thrown, press moulded, and cast.

Born in New Zealand. Trained at Slade School
of Art and Central School of Art. Fellow of
Society of Designer Craftsmen. Work in
Auckland Museum; Wellington Museum;
Christchurch Museum. Exhibitions: 1974,
Wellington and Christchurch. Wrote *Practical
Pottery and Ceramics*, London 1964; *Pottery
Throwing for Beginners*, London 1970. Teaches,
Central School of Art.

Sells direct from workshop.

COLE Tarquin
The Old Brewery, Wishward, Rye TN31 7DH, Sussex
tel: 079 73 3038
visitors welcome to showroom, open normal shop hours

Decorative tile manufacturer, to own or customers' designs.

Born in London. Trained Royal College of Art. Fellow of Royal Society of Arts. Design Council Award Winner, 1966, 1969, 1974. Exhibition: 1975: Rye Art Gallery. See *House and Garden*, July 1975; *Good Housekeeping*, October 1975; *Ideal Home*, October 1975.

Sells from showroom, 12 Connaught Street, London W2 and at Tilemart shops throughout Britain.

COLLYER Ernest
Railway Station House, Winchelsea, Sussex
tel: 079 76 569
visitors welcome at any time

Stoneware pots, vases, candleholders and bird baths, and ceramic confectionery – jam tarts and flans. Also some Raku ware.

Trained with a studio potter. Married to Pamela Nash. Work in Smithsonian Institute, Washington; Herbert Art Gallery, Coventry; Buckinghamshire Education Committee; Inner London Education Authority Collections. Exhibitions (with Pamela Nash): 1970, Oxford Playhouse; 1972, Camden Art Centre; 1974, Rye Art Gallery; 1975, Centaur Gallery, Highgate, Sackville Gallery, East Grinstead. See Jan Arundel, *Exploring Sculpture*, London 1971.

Sells from workshop and Centaur Gallery London; Sackville Gallery.

CONSTANTINIDIS Joanna
2 Bells Chase, Great Baddow, Chelmsford
Essex CM2 8DT
tel: 0245 71842
visitors by appointment – preferably Saturday mornings

Thrown stoneware, usually unglazed, and shaped when leather hard, reduction fired in a gas kiln.

Trained Sheffield College of Art. Member of Craftsmen Potters Association. Exhibitions: 1969, 1973 in Peter Dingley Gallery, Stratford on Avon. Wrote 'Some Techniques' in *Pottery Quarterly*, Spring 1974. Teaches Mid-Essex Technical College. Chelmsford.

Sells from workshop and Primavera; Craftwork; Peter Dingley Gallery; Salix.

COOKSON Delan
5 Mole Run, High Wycombe
Buckinghamshire HP13 5JJ
tel: 0494 34256
visitors by appointment

Decorative ceramic sculpture, in limited editions using a variety of techniques: throwing, turning, extruding, slab building, press moulding. Ceramic murals.

Born Torquay, Devon. Trained Bournemouth College of Art; Central School of Art & Crafts. Fellow of Society of Designer-Craftsmen; Member of Craftsmen Potters Association. 1974 Gold medallist at Vallauris Fourth International Exhibition of Ceramic Art. Exhibition: 1971, Salix, Windsor. Various reviews in *Ceramic Review*. See also *Ceramic Review*, 29, 1974. Teaches full-time, Buckinghamshire College of Higher Education, High Wycombe.

Sells direct and at Collection; Scopas.

COOPER Emmanuel
Fonthill Pottery, 38 Chalcot Road, London NW1
tel: 01-722 9090
visitors by appointment

Domestic oxidised stoneware, and some individual pieces, mostly thrown and all turned on the wheel. Glazes are simple white and opaque.

Member, Society of Designer-Craftsmen; Craftsmen Potters Association. Co-editor of *Ceramic Review*. Exhibition: 1973, Sumas, Windsor. Wrote *Handbook of Pottery*, 1970; *History of Pottery*, 1972; *Taking up Pottery*, 1974; with Eileen Lewenstein, *New Ceramics*, 1974. Teaches part time, Hornsey College of Art.

Sells from workshop and in Boadicea, London.

COPER Hans
c/o Crafts Advisory Committee
12 Waterloo Place, London, SW1Y 4AU

Thrown and hand shaped hollow forms in stoneware. The emphasis is on shape and variety of surface texture. Glazes are matt, in shades of black and white.

Born in Germany. Worked with Lucie Rie before setting up his own workshop in 1958. Gold Medallist, Milan Triennale, 1954. Work in numerous public collections, among them Amsterdam, Stedelijk Museum; National Museum of Wales, Cardiff; Hetjens Museum, Düsseldorf; Kunstmuseum, Hamburg; Museum of Modern Art, Kyoto; Victoria and Albert Museum; Museum of Modern Art, New York; Boymans-van Beuningen Museum, Rotterdam. Numerous exhibitions in Europe, Japan and USA. See M. Rose, *Artist Potters in England*, 1955; Tony Birks, *The Art of the Modern Potter*, 1967; E. Lucie Smith, *The World of the Makers*, 1975.

CROWLEY Jill
401½ Workshops, 401½ Wandsworth Road
London sw8 2JP
tel: 01-622 7262
visitors by appointment

Ceramic sculpture, mainly handbuilt, but also
slip cast and moulded, in Raku and oxidised
stoneware.

Born in Ireland. Trained Royal College of Art.
Teaches part time, Morley College, London.

Sells direct from workshop and at Strangeways,
London; Quadrangle.

DAVEY John
Old Bridge Pottery, Bridge of Dee,
Castle Douglas, Kirkcudbrightshire, Scotland
tel: 055 668 239
visitors welcome 9 am – 5 pm, Monday to Friday

Domestic and decorative stoneware and ceramic
mosaics, thrown, press-moulded and hand-built.
Decoration with brushed pigment, sgraffito, wax
and applied clay.

Born in Nottingham. Studied, Edinburgh
College of Art. Member, Society of Scottish
Artists.

Sells from workshop and in Scottish Craft
Centre; Old Kemble Galleries; Bluecoat Display
Centre.

de TREY Marianne
Shinners Bridge Pottery, Dartington, Totnes,
Devon TQ9 6JB
tel: 080 46 2046
visitors by appointment

Standard ware – pots in oxidised stoneware
mostly for table, and some for flower arranging.
Less functional stoneware is oil and wood fired
and reduced, also porcelain bowls and bottles,
mostly decorated.

Trained at Royal College of Art and in USA.
Member of Craftsmen Potters Association.
Exhibitions: 1971, Boadicea, London; 1972,
Commonwealth Institute; 1974, Craftwork,
Guildford. Work in Victoria and Albert
Museum.

Sells direct from workshop and in Heal's,
London; Craftwork.

DICK Peter
Coxwold Pottery, Coxwold, York YO6 4AA
tel: 034 76 344
visitors welcome 10 am – 5 pm, Monday to Friday

Standard range of earthenware cooking and
tableware, lead glazed (regularly tested for
safety) and unglazed stoneware storage pots and
bowls, wood fired.

Born in London. Trained at Abuja Pottery
Training Centre, Nigeria and Winchcombe
Pottery, Gloucestershire. Member of Craftsmen
Potters Association. Article on 'Slip Decoration'
in *Ceramic Review*, 26, 1974.

Sells direct from workshop and Meander,
Durham, Leeds and Newcastle; Warehouse.

EDMONDS David
45 Devonshire Drive, Greenwich, London SE10
tel: 01-692 8964
visitors by appointment on Monday, Wednesday and Thursday evenings

Slab-built architectural ceramics, usually ash-glazed stoneware.

Trained at Goldsmiths College of Art, where he now teaches. Also teaches at Woolwich Adult Institute for Further Education. Member of Craftsmen Potters Association. See *Ceramics Review*, 34, 1975.

Sells direct from workshop; The Craft Gallery; The Ceramics Shop.

ELLISON Zoë
75 Glisson Road, Cambridge
tel: 0223 59140
visitors by appointment

Earthenware and stoneware, decorative and domestic.

Trained Ewenny Pottery, Glamorgan and Camberwell School of Art. Work in collections of Bristol City Museum; Derby Museum. Teaches at Cambridge School of Art.

Sells from workshop.

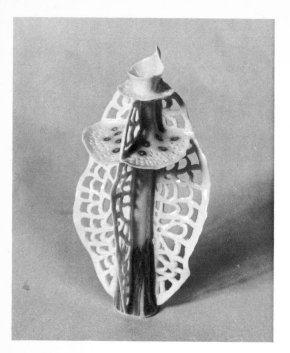

FEIBLEMAN Dorothy
Rose Ghyll Pottery, Rectory Road, Retford,
Nottinghamshire
tel: 0777 4214
visitors by appointment

Inlaid coloured porcelain, pots and jewellery.

Born Indiana, USA. Trained Rochester
Institute of Technology. Numerous awards in
the USA. Work in collections of Orton Cone
Co., Amoco Clay Co., Rochester Institute of
Technology. See *Ceramic Review*, 35, 1975.

Sells direct from workshop and Casson Gallery,
London; Primavera.

FINCH Ray
Winchcombe Pottery, Winchcombe,
Cheltenham GL54 5NU, Gloucestershire
tel: 0242 602462
*visitors welcome 9 am – 5 pm, Monday to Friday and
9 am – 1 pm Saturday*

A wide range of domestic stoneware, mostly
hand-thrown, with lead-free glazes, wood fired.

Born in London. Trained with Michael Cardew
at Winchcombe, which he has run himself since
1945. Member of Craftsmen Potters Association.
Exhibition: 1974, Craftwork, Guildford.

Sells direct from workshop and Casson Gallery
and Group Interiors, London; Interform;
Primavera; Craftwork; Peter Dingley;
Dartington Hall shop.

FRITSCH Elizabeth

Unit 3, Digswell House, Monks Rise,
Welwyn Garden City, Hertfordshire
tel: 96 33375
visitors by appointment

One-off handcoiled vessels in stoneware painted
with slip or glaze, and some slip-cast vessels in
porcelain, spray-glazed.

Born in Wales. Trained Royal College of Art.
Herbert Read Memorial Prize; prize-winner,
Royal Copenhagen Jubilee competition, 1972.
Work in Copenhagen, Kunst-Industrie Museum;
Leeds Museum and Art Gallery. Exhibitions:
1972, Copenhagen; 1974, London, Crafts
Advisory Committee Gallery. See *Crafts*, 10,
1974 and Edward Lucie-Smith, *The Makers*,
1975.

Sells from workshop.

FUCHS Tessa

24 Cross Road, Kingston upon Thames,
Surrey KT2 6HG
tel: 01-549 6906
visitors by appointment

Red earthenware thrown, turned, carved and
assembled to form scenes and features of the
countryside – landscapes, with animals, trees,
people. Coloured glazes are laid over oxides, and
fired in an electric kiln.

Born in Cheshire. Trained Salford Royal
Technical College and Central School of Art &
Crafts. Member, Craftsmen Potters Association.
Exhibitions: 1970, Chagford Galleries, Devon;
1971, Briglin Studio, London; 1972, Salix,
Windsor; 1973, Craftsmen Potters Shop; 1975,
Commonwealth Institute, London. See Michael
Casson, *Pottery in Britain Today*, 1967. Teaches,
Putney School of Art.

Sells from workshop and Best of British,
London; Bluecoat Display Centre.

GANDY Paul
8 Mantilla Drive, Styvechale, Coventry,
Warwickshire
tel: 0203 413052
visitors by appointment

Ceramic stoneware sculpture, ash glazed –
architectural forms and landscapes, extruded,
thrown, slabbed and modelled. Also large thrown
domestic bowls, stoneware fired.

Trained Torquay School of Art and Bretton
Hall, Yorks. Teaches at St Paul's College of
Education, Rugby.

Sells from workshop and Twenty-first century,
London; Minster; Gallery 10½; Bluecoat Display
Centre; Petitte Gallery; Focus; Peter Dingley
Gallery.

GANT Tony
53 Southdean Gardens, Southfields,
London SW19
tel: 01-789 4518
trade enquiries only

Reduction fired stoneware: coffee sets, wine
sets, lidded boxes and vases.

Trained Hammersmith College of Art. Member,
Craftsmen Potters Association.

Sells through Atmosphere; Group Interiors;
Stevens & Capon, London; Primavera;
Studio 10½; Focus Gallery; Nothing; Potipher;
Eef Borger Gallery.

GAYER-ANDERSON John
Ashtree House, Waterbeach, Cambridge
tel: 0223 860421
visitors by appointment

Domestic and decorative earthenware, but work
will not be available until late 1976.

Sells direct to clients.

GILHAM Antony
50A Netherhall Gardens, Hampstead,
London NW3
tel: 01-794 2084
visitors by appointment

Ceramic murals and domestic ware in limited
editions, earthenware, stoneware and porcelain.
Particularly interested in ceramic painting and
murals.

Trained, Central School of Art & Crafts. Work
in collection of Department of the Environment.
Exhibitions: 1969, British Craft Centre; 1971,
Shaw Theatre, London. Teaches, Byam Shaw
School of Painting and Drawing; Goldsmiths
College; Central School of Art & Crafts.

Sells direct from workshop and Best of British,
Bodicea; Heals; Libertys; Strangeways, London

GODFREY Ian
265 Goswell Road, Islington, London EC1
tel: 01-278 5935
visitors by appointment

Individually carved pieces in stoneware with ash glaze.

Member, Craftsmen Potters Association. Work in collection of Victoria & Albert Museum; GLC, London; Bristol City Museum; Glasgow City Museum; Reading Museum; Paisley Museum. Exhibitions: 1970, 1971, 1972, 1973, British Crafts Centre. Teaches, Camberwell School of Art.

Sells through Best of British and Boadicea, London.

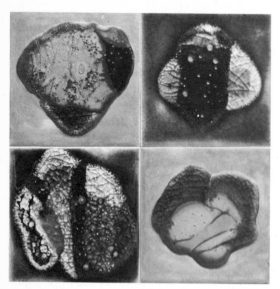

GODFREY Joan
The Studio, Kiln Cottage, Boase Street, Newlyn, Penzance, Cornwall
visitors by appointment

Ceramic tiles with crackle glazes and fused enamel threads. Also majolica tiles.

Trained, Maidenhead Art School. Member, Society of Craftsmen, Hereford; Cornish Society of Craftsmen. Exhibition: 1972, Newlyn Gallery, Newlyn. See Bruce Alexander, *Crafts and Craftsmen*, 1974.

Sells from workshop and Newlyn Gallery, Orion Gallery and Framers Gallery.

HEPBURN Tony
11 Albany Terrace, Leamington Spa,
Warwickshire
tel: 0926 37640
visitors by appointment

Sculptural, partly functional oxidised stoneware,
with some low fire glazes.

Trained, Camberwell School of Art. Work in
Victoria & Albert Museum; ILEA Collection,
London; Hanley Museum, Stoke-on-Trent;
International Museum, Faenza; Takashymya
Gallery, Tokyo. Exhibitions: 1971, Camden
Arts Centre; 1972, Richard Demarco Gallery,
Edinburgh; 1973, Ullman Gallery, Cleveland,
Ohio. See *Ceramic Review*, 13, 1972. Teaches.
Lancaster Polytechnic, Coventry.

Sells from workshop.

HONEY Roger
1 Abbot's Ride, Farnham, Surrey
tel: 025 13 3190
visitors by appointment

Slipcast ceramic objects and sculptures.

Trained, Royal College of Art. Teaches part-
time, West Surrey College of Art and
Goldsmith's College of Art.

Sells direct from workshop and Birmingham
Arts shop.

See *Glass: blown and painted*.

HOY Anita
50 Julian Avenue, Acton, London W3
tel: 01–992 4041
visitors by appointment

Hand thrown domestic and individual pieces:
carved slip and oxide painted red earthenware,
stoneware and porcelain.

Trained, Copenhagen College of Arts and
Crafts. Was Head of Studio Department,
Bullers Ltd, Stoke-on-Trent and Royal Doulton,
Lambeth. Member, Craftsmen Potters
Association; Associate Society of Designer-
Craftsmen; Council of Industrial Design. Work
in Victoria & Albert Museum Collection;
Hanley Museum, Stoke-on-Trent. Teaches,
Hammersmith College of Art; West Surrey
College of Art.

Sells from workshop.

JUPP Mo
Upper Tump Farm, English Bicknor,
Nr Coleford, Gloucestershire
tel: 059 46 727
visitors by appointment

Individual sculptural pieces in reduced
stoneware and other media.

Trained, Royal College of Art. Work in
Victoria & Albert Museum Collection; Crafts
Advisory Committee Collection. Teaches,
Harrow College of Art; West Surrey College of
Art, Farnham; Middlesex Polytechnic, Hornsey.

Sells at workshop.

KEELER Walter
Moorcroft Cottage, Penallt,
Monmouth, Gwent
visitors by appointment

Range of everyday wares in reduced stoneware
and saltglaze, together with small editions of
individual pots in variety of ware including
porcelain.

Member, Craftsmen Potters Association.
Exhibition: 1972, Scopas Gallery, Henley on
Thames. See *Ceramic Review*, 18, 1972.

Sells direct from workshop.

KELLAM Colin
The Lion Brewery, South Street, Totnes, Devon
tel: 0803 863158
visitors by appointment

Reduced stoneware, thrown and slabbed.

Trained, Loughborough College of Art and
with Marianne de Trey. Member, Craftsmen
Potters Association; Devon Guild of Craftsmen.

Sells direct from workshop and Heals, London.

LEACH Bernard

The Leach Pottery Ltd, St Ives, Cornwall
tel: 073 670 6398

Stoneware production and individual pieces; has
not made any pots since 1973.

After studying drawing and etching at the Slade
and London Schools of Art, visited Japan and
took up study of pottery. Established Leach
Pottery with Shoji Hamada at St Ives in 1920,
drawing on traditions and techniques of East and
West. CBE, CH. Awarded Binns Medal, American
Society of Ceramics; Japanese Order of the
Sacred Treasure. Some fifty exhibitions in Japan,
Scandinavia, Europe and United States. Work in
numerous public collections in Europe, Japan
and USA. Wrote *A Potter's Book*, 1st ed. London,
1940; *A Potter in Japan*, London, 1952; *Kenzan
and his Tradition*, London, 1966; *Drawings,
Verses and Belief*, London, 1973.

LEACH David

Lowerdown Pottery, Bovey Tracey, Devon
tel: 0626 833408
*visitors welcome at showroom, 9 am – 6 pm Monday
to Friday; 9 am – 1 pm Saturday*

Mainly handthrown functional domestic ware
and individual stoneware and porcelain.

Trained at Leach Pottery; for ten years was
Bernard Leach's partner. Set up Lowerdown
Pottery in 1956. Gold Medallist, International
Academy of Ceramics Exhibition, Istanbul,
1967. Founder Member of Craftsmen Potters
Association. Work in collection of Exeter
Cathedral; Plymouth City Museum; Victoria &
Albert Museum; Kunstindustrimuseet,
Copenhagen. Exhibitions: 1970, Exeter
University; 1971, City Art Centre Sioux,
Dakota; 1973, Kunstindustrimuseet,
Copenhagen. See *Ceramic Review*, 16, 1972; 21,
1973; 27, 1974.

Sells from workshop; Peter Dingley Gallery.

LEACH Janet
The Leach Pottery Ltd, St Ives, Cornwall
tel: 073 670 6398
visitors by appointment

Stoneware and porcelain production and
individual pieces.

Trained as sculptor and potter in USA. Started
Pottery at Spring Valley, New York in 1949.
Met Bernard Leach in 1952. Exhibitions: 1971,
Tokyo; 1972, London, Marjorie Parr; 1974,
Tenmaya, Okayama; 1975, Amalgam, Barnes;
1976, British Crafts Centre. Work in collection
of Victoria & Albert Museum; Bristol City Art
Gallery; National Museum of Wales, Cardiff;
Bradford City Art Gallery; Museum Boymans,
Rotterdam. See 'Fifty-one years of the Leach
Pottery', *Ceramic Review*, 14, 1972.

Sells Marjorie Parr; Amalgam and Turret
Bookshop, London; and at the Leach Pottery.

LEACH Jeremy
Lowerdown Pottery, Bovey Tracey, Devon
tel: 0626 833 408
*Visitors welcome at showroom, 9 am – 6 pm Monday
to Friday; 9 am – 1 pm Saturday*

Handthrown functional domestic ware, and
chess pieces, some lidded cut-sided pots and
impressed fluted pots, in stoneware or porcelain.

Trained Central School of Art and Camberwell
School of Art and with David Leach. See
Ceramic Review, 21, 1973; 27, 1974.

Sells direct from workshop and the Oxford
Gallery.

LEACH John
Muchelney Pottery, Muchelney, Nr Langport,
Somerset
tel: 0458 250324
*visitors welcome to showroom 9 am – 6 pm Monday
to Friday; 9 am – 1 pm Saturday*

Handthrown domestic stoneware, reduction
fired.

Trained with Bernard and David Leach.
Member, Craftsmen Potters Association.
Exhibitions: 1972, Dillington House, Ilminster;
1974, Aston University, Birmingham. See
Ceramic Review, 18, 1972.

Sells direct from pottery craftshop; in David
Mellor and Heals, London; Friars Gallery;
Athenea.

LEWENSTEIN Eileen
11 Western Esplanade, Hove, Sussex BN4 1WE
tel: 0273 418705
visitors by appointment

Pots and objects in stoneware and porcelain,
pinched, coiled, slab built, press moulded and
thrown.

Trained, West of England College of Art;
Beckenham School of Art; University of
London. Member, International Academy of
Ceramics and Craftsmen Potters Association.
Exhibition: 1971, Pace Gallery, London.
Co-editor, *Ceramic Review;* with Emmanuel
Cooper, *New Ceramics*, 1974. See also *Ceramic
Review*, 4, 1970; 9, 1971; Maria Schofield,
Decorative Art and Modern Interiors, 1975;
*Internationales Keramikessymposium, Mettlach,
Sommer 1974*, Villeroy and Boch, 1975.

Sells direct from workshop and Amalgam and
Casson Gallery, London; Bluecoat Display
Centre.

MABON Robert
Tanglewood, Wilton Lane, Jordans,
Beaconsfield, Buckinghamshire HP9 2RG
tel: 024 07 3189
visitors by appointment

Individual pots, dishes, boxes, sculpture in
stoneware.

For illustration see *Textiles: weaving*.

MALTBY John
Stoneshill Pottery, Stoneshill, Crediton, Devon
tel: 036 32 2753
*visitors welcome 9 am – 5.30 pm Monday to Friday;
9 am – 12.30 pm Saturday*

Small ceramic sculptures in stoneware or
saltglaze and some domestic pots.

Trained, Leicester College of Art; Goldsmiths
College and with David Leach. Member,
Craftsmen Potters Association. Work in Exeter
Museum collection. Exhibitions: 1971, Chagford
Gallery; 1972, Craftwork, Guildford; 1973,
Chagford Gallery; 1974, Primavera, Cambridge.
See *Ceramic Review*, 29, 1974.

Sells direct from workshop and Primavera and
Craftwork.

MARGRIE Victor
c/o Crafts Advisory Committee,
12 Waterloo Place, London SW1Y 4AU
no visitors

Porcelain – individual pieces.

Born in London. Trained, Hornsey College of Art. Fellow, Society of Industrial Artists and Designers; Member, Craftsmen Potters Association; International Academy of Ceramics. Work in Victoria & Albert Museum, London. Exhibitions: 1962, with Michael Casson; 1964, with Sandy Mackilligin at the Crafts Centre of Great Britain. Contributor to the *Oxford Companion to the Decorative Arts*, 1975. See *Ceramic Review*, 19, 1973.

Sells direct to clients.

MATTHEWS Leo
Art Block, College of Art, Technical College, London Road, Shrewsbury, Salop
tel: 0743 51544 Ex 42
visitors by appointment

Architectural murals and sculptural ceramics.

Trained, Manchester College of Art; Stoke-on-Trent College of Art. Fellow, Society of Designer-Craftsmen. Member, Craftsmen Potters Association. Work in Accrington Museum collection; Clive House Museum, Shrewsbury. Teaches full-time, Shrewsbury College of Art.

Sells direct from workshop.

MELLON Eric
5 Parkfield Avenue, Bognor Regis, Sussex
tel: 024 32 2331
visitors by appointment

Stoneware bowls and cylinders with wood ash glazes and mostly brush drawn decoration; all individual pieces.

Trained, Watford School of Art; Harrow School of Art; Central School of Art. Fellow, Society of Designer-Craftsmen. Member, Craftsmen Potters Association. Work in collection of ILEA; Abbot Hall Art Gallery, Kendal; Bishop Otter College; Cumberland Education Authority; Portsmouth City Museum. Exhibitions: 1970, David Paul Gallery, Chichester; Abbot Hall Gallery; 1973, Commonwealth Institute.

Sells from workshop and David Paul Gallery.

NASH Pamels
Railway Station House, Winchelsea, Sussex
tel: 079 76 569
visitors by appointment

Slab built and coiled ceramic pieces, mainly sculptural, and ceramic panels with moveable pieces on magnets, which can be changed around.

Trained, Willesden School of Art; Central School of Art & Crafts. Married to Ernest Collyer. Work in Herbert Art Gallery, Coventry; Borough Museum, Scunthorpe; Museum of Fine Art, Tokyo; Smithsonian Institution, Washington. Exhibitions (with Ernest Collyer): 1970, Oxford Playhouse; 1972, Camden Arts Centre; 1974, Rye Art Gallery; 1975, Centaur Gallery, London and Sackville Gallery, East Grinstead. See Jan Arundel, *Exploring Sculpture*, 1971.

Sells direct from workshop and Asset; Centaur Gallery, London; Sackville Gallery.

NELSON John
Inchmill, Glenprosen, Nr Kirriemuir,
Angus DD8 4SA, Scotland
visitors by appointment

Reduction fired stoneware, and some porcelain
and Raku ware. Large handbuilt planters and
pots a speciality.

Trained, Edinburgh College of Art and
University of Madison, Wisconsin. Member,
Society of Scottish Artists. Work in collection of
Glasgow Art Gallery; Everson Museum,
Syracuse, New York. Teaches, Edinburgh
College of Art.

Sells from workshop and Scottish Craft Centre
and Ian Clarkson Gallery.

NEWMAN Bryan
The Pottery, Aller, Langport, Somerset
tel: 0458-250 244
visitors by appointment

Ceramic sculpture and domestic pottery.

Trained, Camberwell School of Art. Member,
Craftsmen Potters Association. Exhibition: 1970.
Craftsmen Potters Association. See articles in
Pottery Quarterly and M. Casson, *Pottery in
Britain Today;* Tony Birks, *The Art of the
Modern Potter.*

Sells direct from workshop.

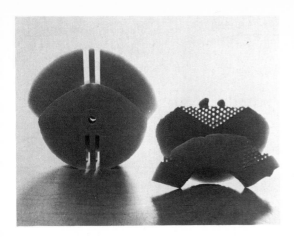

NISBET Eileen
4 Great Ormond Street, Holborn, London WC1
tel: 01-242 7362
no visitors

Large press moulded earthenware dishes with
linear decoration and amber glaze; stoneware
and porcelain tiles and panels, white, blue and
unglazed; small porcelain objects, handbuilt and
pierced, white.

Trained, Central School of Art & Crafts.
Member, Craftsmen Potters Association.
Teaches, Central School of Art & Crafts and
Harrow School of Art.

Sells through Casson Gallery, London.

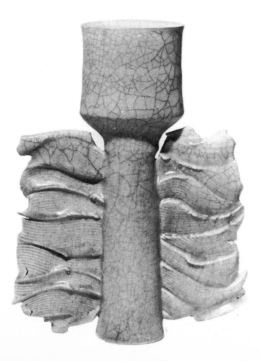

PEARSON Colin
Wickham Lodge, 73 High Street, Aylesford,
Kent
tel: 0622 77916
visitors by appointment

Individual work in porcelain and stoneware, and
a range of tableware in reduced stoneware in
three glazes.

Born in Herefordshire. Trained at Goldsmiths
College, at Winchcombe Pottery and with
David Leach at Aylesford Pottery. 1975, winner
of Premio Faenza. Member, Craftsmen Potters
Association. Work in collection of Victoria &
Albert Museum; Bristol City Museum;
Maidstone Museum; Leicester City Museum;
Portsmouth City Museum; Royal Scottish
Museum, Edinburgh; Glasgow City Museum.
Exhibitions: 1971, Crafts Centre of Great
Britain; 1972, Oxford Gallery (with Peter
Collingwood); 1975, Craftwork, Guildford.
Teaches, Camberwell School of Art; Harrow
School of Art; Medway College of Design.

Sells direct from workshop and Libertys, Casson
Gallery, Atmosphere, London; Craftwork;
Oxford Gallery; Peter Dingley; Greyfriars Art
Shop.

PERRY Sarah
93B Blackheath Road, London SE10
tel: 01-691 3404
visitors by appointment

Individual handbuilt and thrown oxidised
stoneware pieces, mainly bronzed, matt white,
mauve and pink in colour. Also lamps in white
matt glaze, with thrown stems and heads.

Trained, Camberwell School of Art.
Exhibitions: 1972, Shalford Gallery, Guildford;
1973, Sean Kelly, London. See Robert Harling,
Modern Furniture and Decoration, Collins.
Teaches part-time, South Lambeth Adult
Education Institute.

Sells direct from workshop and Affinity,
Atmosphere, Best of British, Boadicea and Sean
Kelly, London; Ralph Lewis; Craft Shop
Flament; European Craft Centre.

PHILP Paul
28 Perrymead Street, London SW6
tel: 01-736 0688
visitors by appointment

Agate ware – experiments with stained clays.

Work in collection of National Museum of
Wales, Cardiff and Welsh Arts Council
collection. Exhibition: 1971, Mason's Yard
Gallery, London. See *Ceramic Review*, 13, 14,
1972; 21, 23, 1973. Teaches part-time, Central
School of Art & Crafts and Bath Academy of
Art.

Sells direct from workshop and Strangeways,
London.

PLEYDELL BOUVERIE Katharine
Kilmington Manor, Warminster,
Wiltshire BA12 6RD
tel: 098 53 259
visitors by appointment

Mainly middle temperature ash glazed pots and
bowls, individual pieces.

Trained, Central School of Art and Crafts and
Leach Pottery. Member, Craftsmen Potters
Association. Work in collection of British
Museum; Victoria & Albert Museum;
University College of Wales, Aberystwyth;
Hanley Museum, Stoke-on-Trent and many
other collections. Exhibitions: 1974, Selwood
Galleries, Frome; 1976, Casson Gallery, London.
See *Ceramic Review*, 28, 30, 1974; *Crafts*, 19,
1976.

Sells at Casson Gallery, London.

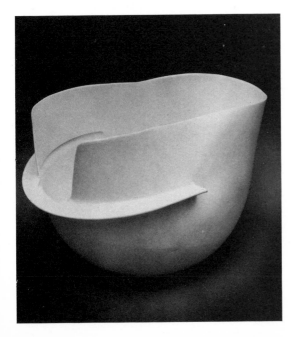

PONCELET Jacqueline
145 Pancras Road, London NW1
tel: 01-387 6230
visitors by appointment

Handcarved fine bone china, individual pieces.

Trained, Wolverhampton College of Art and
Royal College of Art. Work in Victoria &
Albert Museum; Edinburgh, Royal Scottish
Museum; Glasgow, Museum; Portsmouth, City
Museum; Southampton, City Museum;
Reading Museum; Vestlandske
Kunstindustrimuseum, Bergen;
Nationalmuseum, Stockholm. See *Brides*,
September, 1975. Teaches part-time, West
Surrey College of Art, Farnham and
Portsmouth Polytechnic.

Sells direct from workshop and Casson Gallery,
Liberty's, London; Oxford Gallery.

REYCHAN Stanislas
Garden Studio, 3 Acacia Road, London NW8
tel: 01-722 1285
visitors welcome any time

Individual ceramic figures and ornaments, modelled in rolled and pressed clay.

Trained, St Martin's School of Art and Central School of Art & Crafts. MBE. Member, Craftsmen Potters Association; National Society of Painters, Sculptors and Printers. See *Arts Review*, April, 1974.

Sells direct from workshop and Society of Craftsmen, Hereford; Bluecoat Display Centre; North West Arts Association.

RICHARDSON Andrew
Little Bubhurst Farm, Frittenden, Cranbrook, Kent
tel: 058 080 233
visitors by appointment

Domestic ware in earthenware and stoneware, some salt glazed pieces. Also Raku pots, slab-built castles and villages, and porcelain.

Trained, Harrow School of Art. Member, Craftsmen Potters Association. Work in collection of Victoria & Albert Museum. See E. Cooper and E. Lewenstein, *New Ceramics*, 1974.

Sells direct from workshop and Casson Gallery, London; Craftwork; Sackville Gallery; John Pierce; Potipher; Athenea; Pottenbakker.

RIE Lucie
c/o Crafts Advisory Committee,
12 Waterloo Place, London SW1Y 4AU

Stoneware and porcelain, thrown and shaped
hollow ware, with matt glazes, rough surface
and very little colour.

Born in Vienna. Trained, Kunstgewerbe Schule;
came to England in 1938. Numerous exhibitions
in Britain, Europe and USA, several jointly with
Hans Coper. Work in many public collections.
Major retrospective exhibition 1967; 1970, 1971,
Marjorie Parr, London; 1970, Expo '70, Osaka;
National Museum of Modern Art, Kyoto; 1971,
Bradford City Gallery; Primavera, Cambridge;
Kettle's Yard, Cambridge; 1972, Hamburg
Museum of Art & Craft; 1974, Dusseldorf,
Hetjens Museum. Gold medallist Munich
International Exhibition, 1964. See L. W.
Rochowanski, *Wiener Keramik*, Thyrsos,
Vienna, 1923; G. W. Digby, *The Work of the
Modern Potter in England*, 1952; M. Rose, *Artist
Potters in England*, 1955; M. Casson, *Pottery in
England Today*, 1967; E. Lucie Smith, *The World
of the Makers*, 1975; *Ceramic Review*, 27, 1974.

ROBINSON David
5 Clare Road, Cotham, Bristol BS6 5TB, Avon
visitors by appointment

Ceramic sculpture in reduced stoneware.

Trained, Sunderland College of Art and Royal
College of Art. Work in collection of Bristol
Schools Art Service; Portsmouth City Museum;
Southampton Art Gallery; Exeter Museum. See
Griselda Lewis, *A Collector's History of English
Pottery*, London, 1969. Teaches, Bristol
Polytechnic.

Sells direct from workshop.

ROBINSON Joyce
Murtle Station, Bieldside, Aberdeen AB1 9EQ
tel: 0224 48963
visitors by appointment

Trained, Central School of Art. Fellow, Society
of Designer-Craftsmen; Member, International
Academy of Ceramics. Work in collection of
Staffordshire Education Authority.

Sells direct from workshop.

ROGERS Mary
Brook Farm House, Nanpantan Road,
Loughborough, Leicestershire
tel: 0509 39205
visitors by appointment

Hand modelled individual pieces in porcelain
and stoneware.

Fellow, Society of Designer-Craftsmen.
Member, International Academy of Ceramics
and Craftsmen Potters Association. Work in
collection of British Council; Crafts Advisory
Committee; ILEA; Derbyshire Museum
Service; Nottingham City Art Gallery;
Bradford City Art Gallery. Exhibitions: 1972,
Peter Dingley, Stratford on Avon; 1974, Oxford
Gallery; 1975, British Crafts Centre. See
Ceramic Review, 9, 1971; 38, 1976 and E. Cooper
and E. Lewenstein, *New Ceramics*, 1974; Tony
Birks, *The Potter's Companion*, 1974.

Sells direct from workshop and Casson Gallery,
London; Oxford Gallery; Peter Dingley
Gallery; Andrée Samson Gallery.

ROMPALA Elizabeth
1 Charlwood Road, Putney, London SW15
tel: 01-788 8666
visitors by appointment

Mostly abstract individual handbuilt forms, stoneware and porcelain; some functional pieces.

Trained, St Martin's School of Art; Putney School of Art. Work in collection of Leicestershire Education Committee; Ministry of Public Building and Works. Exhibition: 1972, Salix, Windsor. Teaches part-time, Wandsworth.

Sells from workshop and Salix.

SIMMONDS Clive
Brettenham Ceramics, B25 The Forge, Brettenham, Ipswich, Suffolk IP7 7QP
tel: 044 93 620
visitors welcome any time

Ceramic tiles, multicoloured, with inlaid glazes, sold singly or made up into panels for murals.

Trained, Norwich School of Art; Bournemouth and Poole School of Art.

Sells direct from workshop and Cornwall Crafts; Field Art Studio.

SIMPSON Peter
Riccione, Manchester Road, Sway,
Lymington, Hampshire
tel: 059 08 2147
visitors by appointment

Non-functional ceramics, hand built, pinched,
coiled, pressed with some slip casting, in
porcelain and porcelain/crank mix.

Trained, Bournemouth and Poole College of
Art. Fellow, Society of Designer-Craftsmen and
Society of Industrial Artists and Designers. Work
in Victoria & Albert Museum; Bradford City
Art Gallery; Royal Scottish Museum,
Edinburgh; Leicester Museum; Portsmouth
Museum Schools Service. Exhibitions: 1970, Pace
Gallery, London; 1972, Alicat, London; 1973,
Primavera, Cambridge; 1974, British Crafts
Centre. See *Ceramic Review*, 4, 1970; 15, 1972;
20, 1973; 23, 1973; 25, 1974; *Crafts Horizons*,
1973; *Crafts*, July, September, 1973; January,
July, November, 1974. E. Cooper and
E. Lewenstein, *New Ceramics*, 1974. Teaches,
Bristol Polytechnic.

Sells direct from workshop and Casson Gallery,
London; Oxford Gallery; Galerie Köster;
Galerie Noella Gest.

SMITH Martin
Coles Farm, Valley Road, Buxhall,
Nr Stowmarket, Suffolk
tel: 0449 720601 (evenings)
visitors by appointment

Mostly hand thrown individual pieces, turned
and bisque fired, Raku glaze fired. Some
sculptural work.

Trained, Bristol Polytechnic and Royal College
of Art. Exhibition: 1975, David Durant
Gallery, Bristol. Wrote article, 'Raku
Techniques' in *Crafts*, September, 1974.

Sells direct from workshop and Casson Gallery,
London.

SOLLY John
36 London Road, Maidstone, Kent ME16 8QL
tel: 0622 546
visitors welcome at any time

Hand-thrown domestic repetition and
individual pots in red and buff sanded clays,
slipware and high-fired earthenware.

Trained, Camberwell and Central Schools of
Art with short working periods at Rye and
Winchcombe potteries. Fellow, Royal Society
of Arts; Society of Designer-Craftsmen;
founder member, Craftsmen Potters
Association. Teaches, Folkestone Adult
Education Centre and runs own summer school
at the pottery.

Sells from workshop.

STERCKX Anthony
The Afandale, Cymmer, Nr Port Talbot,
West Glamorgan
tel: 063 983 591
visitors welcome any time

Domestic pots, Ikebana pots, lamp bases, plant
containers, and murals and large sculptures, all
thrown or slab built in stoneware, earthenware
or terracotta, generally with local wood ash
glazes.

Trained, Hereford and Camberwell Colleges of
Art. Member, Craftsmen Potters Association.
Work in collections of Hereford City Museum;
Oxford County Museum; Sheffield University.
Exhibition: 1970, Sheffield University.

Sells direct from workshop and Books and
Crafts; Handmade; Peter Dingley.

SWINDELL Geoffrey
11 Mark Street, Riverside, Cardiff,
South Glamorgan
tel: 0222 35010
visitors by appointment

Press moulded or wrap-around porcelain substructures with various extra parts moulded or hand modelled – glazes are pastel colours with occasional sand blasted surface or on-glaze lustre or liquid metal details.

Trained, Stoke-on-Trent College of Art; Royal College of Art. Member, Craftsmen Potters Association. Work in collection of Reading Museum; Bradford City Art Gallery. Exhibitions: 1972, British Crafts Centre; 1974, Oxford Gallery; Midland Group Gallery, Nottingham; Sutton College, Surrey. See *Ceramic Review*, 18, 1972; 19, 1973; 27, 1974; 34, 1975; *Crafts*, September, 1974; *Brides*, September, 1975. Teaches, Cardiff College of Art.

Sells from workshop and Casson Gallery, London; Oxford Gallery.

TAYLOR Stuart
401½ Workshops, 401½ Wandsworth Road, London SW8 2JP
tel: 01-622 7261/2
visitors welcome after 3 pm Monday to Friday; Saturday 11 am – 3 pm

Individual hand thrown stoneware pieces, fired in oxidised atmosphere and cast white earthenware decorated with silkscreen enamel transfers and lustre, to commission or in small, strictly limited editions.

Trained, Camberwell School of Art; Royal College of Art.

Sells direct from workshop.

TCHALENKO Janice
30 Therapia Road, East Dulwich, London SE22
tel: 01-693 1624
visitors by appointment

Hand thrown domestic ware in reduced stoneware, including teapots, coffee sets, casseroles, oven and table wares.

Trained, Harrow School of Art. Member, Craftsmen Potters Association. Teaches, Camberwell School of Art; Croydon College of Art.

Sells Anvil, London; Craftwork; Potipher.

THOMPSON Peter
9 Cherry Walk, Lower Peover, Nr Knutsford, Cheshire
visitors by appointment

Sculptural pieces using ceramic materials and techniques combined with other material, exploring contemporary themes (advertising), natural phenomena and landscape.

Trained, Manchester College of Art. Fellow, Society of Designer-Craftsmen. Work in collection of Hereford County Council; North West Arts Association, Manchester; Salford Museum. Exhibitions: 1971, Birly Gallery, Didsbury College of Education; 1972, Salford Museum. See Isla Moodie, ed. *Decorative Art and Modern Interiors 1973-4*, 1974. Teaches, Padgate College of Education, Warrington, Lancs.

Sells direct from workshop.

WARD John
65 Priolo Road, Charlton, London SE7 7PX
tel: 01-858 6286
visitors by appointment

Individual bowls and pots, handbuilt in
stoneware by pinching and coiling, glazed with
matt glazes.

Trained, Camberwell School of Art. Member,
Craftsmen Potters Association. Exhibition: 1974
Amalgam, London. Teaches, Sydenham and
Forest Hill Adult Education Institute.

Sells direct from workshop and Amalgam,
London; Peter Dingley Gallery.

WELCH Robin
Robin Welch Pottery, Stradbroke, Diss,
Norfolk IP21 5JP
tel: 037 984 416
visitors welcome at any time

Standard production range of domestic
stoneware, part-glazed in semi-matt ash glazes,
most of which is moulded, the rest hand thrown.
Also individual sculptural pieces and panels.

Trained, Nuneaton, Penzance and Central
Schools of Art. CAC Bursary 1976. Member,
Craftsmen Potters Association. Work in
collection of Victoria & Albert Museum; GLC
Collection, London; Exeter Museum;
Leicestershire County Council Education
Department; National Gallery of Victoria,
Melbourne; Art Gallery of New South Wales,
Sydney. Exhibition: 1975, British Crafts
Centre.

Sells Heals, London; Forum; Primavera;
Robert Kelly; Malcolm Bishop; Oxford Gallery.

WHALLEY Anne and Theodore
Haverfordwest Pottery, Clay Lanes,
Haverfordwest SA61 1UH, Dyfed
tel: 0437 2611
visitors by appointment

Thrown individual pieces and tableware in
glazed stoneware.

Trained, City of Birmingham Polytechnic.
Members of Small Potteries Trade Association;
South Wales Potters; Society of Craftsmen,
Hereford. Work in National Museum of Wales,
Cardiff.

Sell direct to clients.

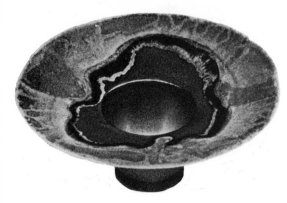

WHITE Mary
Old Castle House & Gallery, The Triangle,
Malmesbury, Wiltshire
tel: 066 62 2448
visitors by appointment

Mainly porcelain – individual pieces with
coloured glazes and some lustre. Specialises in
teapots, bowls and lidded jars.

Born in Wales. Trained, Hammersmith College
of Art; Newport College of Art; Goldsmiths
College, London University. Member of
Society of Scribes and Illuminators; Craftsmen
Potters Association; Society of Designer-
Craftsmen; South Wales Potters. Exhibitions:
1973, Commonwealth Art Gallery; 1974,
Heals; 1975, Bohun Gallery; Salix, Windsor.

Sells direct to clients; Boadicea, Casson Gallery,
Atmosphere, Heals, London; Bohun Gallery;
Bluecoat Display Centre; Gallery 24; Things
Welsh.

**WOODCOCK David and
WOODCOCK-BECKERING Diana**
Crich Pottery, Market Place, Crich,
Nr Matlock, Derbyshire DE4 5DD
tel: 077 385 3171
visitors by appointment

Round tiles, dishes, vases, spherical forms with
graphic interpretation of landscape obtained
with sgraffito and hand painting.

Trained, Loughborough College of Art; Royal
College of Art. Members of Midland Group.
Exhibitions: Calouste Gulbenkian Gallery,
Newcastle-upon-Tyne; 1971, Laing Gallery,
Newcastle-upon-Tyne, Wolverhampton
Polytechnic; 1975, Braithwaite Dunn,
Nottingham, Lantern Gallery.

Sell direct to clients; Heals, Collection, London;
Craftsmens Gallery; Lantern Gallery; Northern
Artists; Yew Tree Gallery; Gallery 359;
Braithwaite & Dunn; The Craft Centre,
Derbyshire; Art Mart.

WOODS Michael
Northridge, Northway, Godalming, Surrey
tel: 048 68 6306
visitors by appointment

Thrown bowls and vases – slab work including
ceramic fountains and small display tables –
bowls with cut lettering.

Trained, Norwich Art School; Slade School of
Fine Art. Exhibition: 1974, Lantern Gallery.
Director of Art at Charterhouse, Surrey.

Sells direct to clients.

WREN Rosemary
The Oxshott Pottery, Potters Croft,
Oakshade Road, Oxshott, Surrey
tel: 970 2485
visitors by appointment

Hollow-built, individually made animals and
birds in stoneware – sometimes porcelain.

Trained, Guildford School of Art; Royal
College of Art. Fellow, Society of Designer-
Craftsmen; Member, Craftsmen Potters
Association Council; International Academy of
Ceramics. Work in Victoria & Albert Museum;
Crafts Museum, Stuttgart. Exhibition: 1968,
Craftsmen Potters Association.

Sells direct to clients; Boadicea, London; Salix.

WYNNE MORRIS John
Conwy Pottery, 8 Castle Street, Conwy,
North Wales
tel: 049 263 3487
visitors by appointment

Thrown domestic stoneware.

Trained, North Staffordshire Polytechnic;
Liverpool Polytechnic. Fellow of the Royal
Society of Arts. Exhibition: 1969, Ceramic
Sculpture, Bangor University.

Sells direct from workshop; Bluecoat Display
Centre; Romanis.

ZADE Anne
16 Oak Way, Crawley, Sussex
tel: 0293 24996
visitors by appointment

Domestic ware and decorative pieces – usually in stoneware, thrown and decorated.

Born in Germany. Trained, Kunst und Gewerbeschule, Hamburg. Member, Guild of Sussex Craftsmen; Society of Designer-Craftsmen. Exhibition: 1973, Horsham Museum, Horsham.

Sells direct to clients; Forty Gallery; Kanya Crafts; Granary Crafts.

ZELINSKI Pauline
4 St Andrews Road, Exwick, Exeter, Devon
tel: 0392 52526
visitors by appointment

Slip-cast forms – functional and non-functional, also some thrown studio pottery.

Trained, West Surrey College of Art and Design, Farnham. Work in The International Museum of Ceramics, Faenza, Italy; Reading Museum. Teaches, Epsom School of Art and Design.

Sells direct to clients; Town Mills Craft Centre; Forum Gallery.

Textiles: batik and fabric printing

BASTICK Fianne
16 Drayson Mews, London w8
tel: 01-937 5662
visitors by appointment

Fabric printing – small runs of printed fabrics, special co-ordinated fashion projects, individual interior commissions. Hand-painted fashion range.

Trained, Hornsey College of Art and Royal College of Art.

Sells direct to clients and through General Trading Company, Pacific 7 and Wardrobe, London; Hattie.

BLOYE Juliet
43 Belgrave Road, London sw1
tel: 01-828 1331
visitors, telephone for appointment

Intricate pictorial batiks on fine silk, often religious or allegorical subjects. A carefully controlled sequence of dye batiks builds up layers of colour and wax until an intricate web of cracks covers the design.

Born in London. Trained, Caulfield & Melbourne Technical College, Australia; studied with Stuart Devlin and Ken Jack. Member, Society of Designer-Craftsmen. Work in Inner London Education Authority collection. Exhibitions: 1970, Roy Hodges Gallery, Greenwich and Hintlesham Festival; 1972, Roy Hodges Gallery; 1974, Snape Craft Gallery, Suffolk. See *Crafts*, September, 1973.

Sells direct to clients.

BOSENCE Susan
Sigford, Bickington, Newton Abbot,
South Devon
tel: 062 682 432
visitors by appointment

Hand block printed cottons, linens and silks.
Resist-dyed cloths in indigo, iron and other
natural dyes. Block printing; also uses resist
dyeing patterns in a variety of methods – wax,
paste, tie, stitch and pleat resists in chemical and
natural dyestuffs.

Self-taught following Barron and Larcher.
Awarded CAC bursary 1975. Work in Victoria
& Albert Museum, London; collection of
Craft Study Centre Trust. Teaches, Camberwell
School of Art; Farnham School of Art; College
of Arts, Dartington.

Sells direct to clients.

CADY Anna
Cala, 27 Warkworth Street, Cambridge.
tel: 0223 65802
visitors by appointment

Wallhangings, weaving and batik using natural
dyes.

Born in Surrey. Trained at West Surrey
College of Art and Design. Farnham. Work in
collection of Reading Museum. Exhibition:
1974, Cambridge Arts and Leisure Association.
Teaches, Cambridge College of Art and
Technology, in own workshop.

Sells direct to clients.

See *Textiles: weaving.*

CAMERON Harriet
3 Fielding Road, Hammersmith, London W14
tel: 01-602 2111 or 01-603 4811
visitors by appointment

Handpainted silk in lengths for scarves and fringed shawls.

Born in London. Trained, Wimbledon School of Art in stained glass. 1965, 1st prize, Royal Worshipful Company of Glaziers Competition; 1967, scholarship awarded by French Government through the British Council.

Sells at Lucienne's, Feathers, Harrods, Fortnum and Mason, Parkers, London; Dorcas Hardin.

DYRENFORTH Noël
11 Shepherds Hill, Highgate, London N6
tel: 01-348 0956
visitors by appointment

Batik – resist method of dyeing and decorating fabric, in panels or stuffed and stitched as sculptural pieces.

Born in London. Member, Society of Designer-Craftsmen. Work in collection of Victoria & Albert Museum; Bradford City Art Gallery; Greater London Council; Crafts Advisory Committee; Devon County Council. Exhibitions: 1970, Herbert Art Gallery, Coventry; Loughborough College of Art; 1971, Heals, London; Oxford Gallery; 1973, Gallery 359, Nottingham; Oxford Gallery; 1975, Atmosphere, London. See John Houston, *Batik with Noël Dyrenforth*, Orbis, 1975.

Sells direct to clients and Atmosphere, London; Oxford Gallery.

HOLDEN Veronica

41 Holmdene Avenue, Herne Hill,
London SE24 9LB
tel: 01-733 8630
visitors by appointment

Fabric printing and printing with airbrush and spray gun – Shibori patterns on wool, silk and cotton for wallhangings, scarves, dress lengths and furnishings – using natural and synthetic dyes.

Trained, Camberwell School of Art; Institute of Education, London University.

Sells direct to clients and Catherine Buckley, London.

HURT Michael

8 Randolph Road, London W9
tel: 01-286 9393
visitors by appointment

Batik – individual wallhangings.

Born in Vancouver, Canada. Self-taught.

Sells from Bayswater Road Market, London; and direct to clients.

KEMP Susan
Millbank Stables, Eyemouth,
Berwickshire TD14 5RE, Scotland
tel: 039 02 306
visitors by appointment

Print designs – wallpapers, wrapping papers,
dress and furnishing fabrics. Print production –
mainly furnishing fabrics but some
commissioned fashion work.

Trained at Goldsmiths College in embroidery
and Royal College of Art, in printed textiles.
Several embroideries in collection of Yorkshire
Education Authority.

Sells at Heals, General Trading Company,
Boadicea (miniature embroideries), London.

See *Textiles: knitting and crochet.*

LAWSON Diana
Woodland Leaves, Cold Ash, Newbury,
Berkshire
tel: 0635 63258
visitors by appointment

Batik pictures and greetings cards. Also
undertakes oriental rug restoration.

Trained, West Surrey College of Art, Farnham
in woven textiles.

Sells direct to clients.

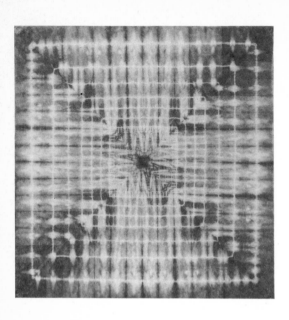

MAILE Anne
29 Horniman Drive, Forest Hill,
London SE23 3BJ
tel: 01-699 9157
no visitors

Tie-dyeing of fabric and paper – wallhangings, panels and collages. Also made-up garments and models in paper. At the present time mostly concerned with publications.

Fellow, Society of Designer-Craftsmen. Work in collections of Reading and Leicestershire Education Committees; Dylon International Ltd and various schools and colleges. Loan exhibitions sent to Training Colleges all over the country from 1960 onwards. Publications, *Tie-and-dye as a Present-day Craft*, London, 1963; *Tie-and-dye Made Easy*, 1971, 1974; *Tie-dyed Paper*, 1975; two articles in *Art & Craft in Education*, November and December, 1975.

Not selling at present.

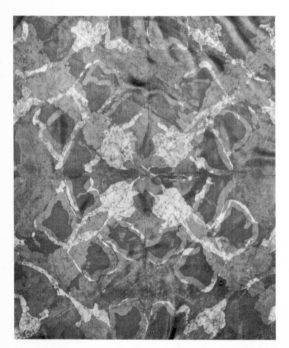

MILES Tamara
Great Hollands Farm, Mollands Lane,
South Ockendon, Essex
tel: 01-700 2347
no visitors

Batik on silk scarves and cotton hangings.

Trained, Chelsea School of Art and Camberwell School of Art.

Sells at Longleat and Mary Loe.

O'CONNELL Michael
The Chase, Perry Green, Much Hadham,
Hertfordshire
tel: 027 984 2689
visitors by appointment

Batik murals.

Studied the primitive techniques of the craft in
various countries. Member, Society of
Industrial Artists and Designers and Society of
Designer-Craftsmen. Work in Victoria &
Albert Museum and in the collections of
Derbyshire, Hertfordshire, Lancashire and
Bedfordshire County Councils. Has had
one-man exhibitions in England, USA, France,
Switzerland, Italy, Australia, New Zealand and
South Africa. Written *Craft Dyeing*, United
Africa House for West African Countries, 1961;
Resist Dyeing and Craft Dyeing, United Africa
Company Textiles, 1962. Teaches at own
studio.

Sells direct to clients and Copper Kettle Gallery.

SICHER Anne
72 Finlay Street, London sw6
tel: 01-385 0338
visitors by appointment

Painting on silk – scarves, men's ties, dress
lengths, shawls, wallhangings.

Born in Paris. Trained, Ecole Supérieure des
Arts Appliqués Dupérre; Ecole Nationale des
Beaux-Arts.

Sells direct to clients and in London, Quadrangle
Gallery; Liberty's; Lucienne's; General Trading
Company; Harrods; Chic of Hampstead.

STUART-WORTLEY Carola
The Beeches, Wilderley, Pulver Batch,
Nr Shrewsbury, Salop
visitors by appointment

Printed textiles for fashion garments.

Born in Kent. Trained at Chelsea School of Art
and Royal College of Art. Teaches at
Wolverhampton Polytechnic.

Sells direct to clients.

ANWYL Doris
2 Lawn Close, Tenterden, Kent
tel: 058 06 2491
visitors by appointment

Various methods of embroidery, particularly collage.

Trained at Croydon School of Art. Fellow, Society of Designer-Craftsmen.

Sells direct to clients.

BALL Mary
22 Vanbrugh Hill, London SE3
tel: 01-858 2942
visitors by appointment

Collage embroideries – panels and wallhangings. Knitted and woven hangings and constructions.

Trained at Goldsmiths College. Member, 62 Group of the Embroiderers' Guild. Teaches, Trent Park College of Education.

Sells direct to clients.

BERTHON Bernard
The Tapestry & Silver Workshop,
Bow Street, Langport, Somerset
visitors by appointment

Canvas work, mainly in geometric designs, for
wall panels, jackets and waistcoats.

Member, Society of Designer-Craftsmen;
Somerset Guild of Craftsmen. Exhibition, 1973,
Dove Centre, Gloucestershire. Teaches at the
Dove Centre of Creativity.

Sells direct to clients.

BINNS Jackie
Hillside Cottage, Horton Corner, Small Dole,
Nr Henfield, Sussex
tel: 0903 814470
visitors by appointment

Embroidery in canvas and leather often made up
into belts and boxes.

For illustration see *Metal: jewellery*.

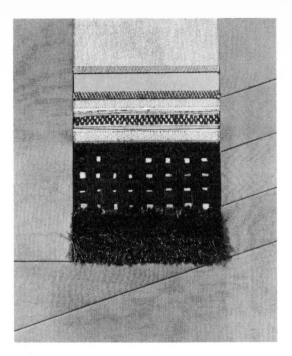

BUTLER Anne
10 Belfield Road, Didsbury,
Manchester M20 0BH
tel: 061 445 7021
visitors by appointment

Abstract embroidery, using hand and machine embroidery.

Born in India. Trained at Bradford College and Goldsmiths College. Fellow, Society of Designer–Craftsmen. Work in the collections of several Education Authorities. Exhibitions: 1970, London; 1971 and 1972, Australia. Publications, six articles in *Art and Craft in Education*, 1974; with Brian French, *Practice of Collage*, 1975; *Simple Machine Embroidery*, 1976. Teaches, Manchester Polytechnic.

Sells direct to clients.

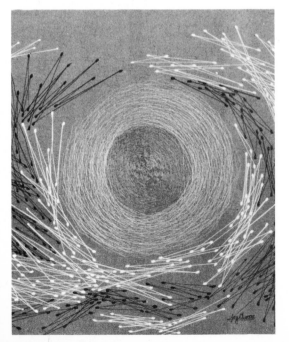

CLUCAS Joy
66 Lexden Road, Colchester, Essex
tel: 0206 42970
visitors by appointment

Abstract wallhangings and panels in applied fabrics and threads and machine embroidery. Dress embroidery to commission.

Born in Hampshire. Trained, Southampton College, Bromley College of Art; Brighton College of Art. Member, 62 Group of the Embroiderers' Guild and Society of Designer–Craftsmen. Work in Victoria & Albert Museum; Shipley Art Gallery; National Museum of Scotland; collection of Embroiderers' Guild; collections of Derby, Reading, Leicester, London, Surrey, Oxford Education Authorities. Exhibitions: 1970, University of Surrey and University of Sussex; 1971, Easter Fair, Johannesburg; 1972, The Minories, Colchester; 1974, Three Households Gallery, Hertfordshire; St Helier, Jersey; 1975, Doncaster College of Art, Central Library, Romford. Publication, *Your Machine for Embroidery*, 1973; series of twelve articles for *Fashion Maker*, 1975. Teaches, Chelmsford County High School and Royal School of Needlework.

Sells direct to clients.

DAWSON Barbara
27 Dartmouth Hill, Greenwich,
London SE10 8AJ
tel: 01-691 3038
visitors by appointment

Various methods of embroidery, particularly
metal thread embroidery for church vestments
and hangings, also hangings in canvas work.

Born in London. Trained, Royal School of
Needlework; Hornsey College of Art;
Goldsmiths College. Member, Society of
Designer-Craftsmen. Work in collections of
many Education Committees and in
Chelmsford Cathedral and chapels at
Cambridge University. Exhibitions: 1973,
Embroiderers' Guild; 1974, Stockwell College of
Education. Publication, *Metal Thread
Embroidery*, 1969. Teaches at Goldsmiths
College.

Sells direct to clients.

DELEVORYAS Lillian
Weatherall Workshops, Weatherall, Coleford,
Gloucestershire GL16 8QB
tel: 059 43 2102
visitors by appointment

Canvas work and appliqué – carpets,
wallhangings, curtains, chairs, cushions,
garments, tile murals, appliqué murals.

Born in Massachusetts, USA. Trained at Pratt
Institute, New York in art and costume design;
at Cooper Union, New York in painting,
drawing, sculpture, printmaking; one year in
Japan and France studying calligraphy and
woodblock printing. Exhibitions: 1972, 401½
Workshops, London; 1973, Colet House,
London; 1975, Clearwell Castle, Gloucestershire,
Regional Craft Centre, Lincoln, Weatherall
Gallery; 1976, Browns, London. See Edward
Lucie-Smith, *The World of the Makers*. Teaches,
at own workshop.

Sells direct to clients.

DMYTRENKO Rene
11 King Street South, Rochdale, Lancashire
visitors by appointment

Quilting, appliqué, canvas work, machine embroidery, patchwork – quilts, bedspreads, cushions, hangings, mirror frames, panels using satins, cottons, shetland wool. Canvas work panels are of shop fronts and houses worked from photographs. Appliquéd lengths are made up of strips of different coloured fabrics joined and decorated with applied shapes.

Trained, Rochdale College of Art; Manchester Polytechnic. Published article in *Embroidery*, Spring 1976. Teaches, Sowerby Bridge Adult Education College, Hyde Technical College.

Sells direct to clients.

See *Textiles: knitting and crochet.*

FASSETT Kaffe
62 Fordwych Road, London NW2
tel: 01-452 3786
visitors by appointment

Canvas work panels, chairs, carpets and cushions, in many types of yarn and many subtle colours. Designs usually of a fanciful nature and figurative.

For illustration see *Textiles: knitting and crochet.*

FRYD Olivia
55 The Crescent, Westbury-on-Trym,
Bristol BS9 4RU
tel: 0272 628726
visitors by appointment

Framed and unframed textile murals –
architectural forms and abstract designs.

Fellow, Society of Designer-Craftsmen. Work
in the collections of Derbyshire and Sussex
Education Authorities.

Sells direct to clients.

GOFFIN Lucy
15 St John's Wood Terrace, London NW8 6JJ
tel: 01-722 2363
visitors by appointment

Quilting and patchwork – boxes decorated with
embroidery, porcelain, silver, leather, pleating,
quilting – patchwork quilts – jackets,
embroidered, quilted, pleated – rag dolls,
approximately 10 ins high.

Born in Buckinghamshire. Trained,
Hammersmith College of Art; Harrow College
of Art; and in apprenticeship with Michael
Casson. Work in Reading Museum.
Exhibition: 1973, British Crafts Centre, with
Mo Jupp. Teaches, West Surrey College of Art,
Farnham.

Sells direct to clients; Casson Gallery,
London; Craftwork.

HARRISON Diana
401½ Workshops, 401½ Wandsworth Road,
London sw8 2JP
tel: 01-622 7261/2
visitors by appointment

Spray dyed, geometric designs on satin, giving
three-dimensional illusions. Fabric quilted and
made up in to furnishings such as bedspreads,
hangings, panels, cushions, curtains.

Born in London. Trained, Goldsmiths College of
Art; Royal College of Art. 1972, Sandersons
award for travel; 1973, Courtaulds textile prize.
Work at Brunel University, Middlesex.
Teaches, Mid-Warwickshire College of Further
Education; West Surrey College of Art,
Farnham.

Sells direct to clients.

HEAD Joyce
34 Bealing Close, Bassett, Southampton,
Hampshire
tel: 0703 67813
visitors by appointment

Fabric collage with hand and machine stitchery
to create interesting surface textures and flat
pattern.

Born in Monmouth. Trained, Great Yarmouth
College of Art; Southampton College of Art.
Work at Southampton University; in
collection of Derbyshire Education Authority.
Teaches, Southampton College of Art.

Sells direct to clients.

HELSDON Maureen
17 Welbeck Avenue, Highfield, Southampton,
Hampshire
tel: 0703 556008
visitors by appointment

Fabric collage with machine embroidery and
screen printing.

Born in London. Trained, Hornsey College of
Art. Fellow, Society of Designer-Craftsmen.
Work in collections of Leicester, Yorkshire,
Southampton Education Authorities and in
collection of Embroiderers' Guild. Exhibition:
1970, Alwin Gallery. Teaches, Southampton
College of Art.

Sells direct to clients.

HOWARD Constance
43 Cambridge Road South, Chiswick,
London W4 3DA
tel: 01-994 3500
visitors by appointment

Wallhangings in appliqué and embroidery,
usually large scale for public buildings and for
ecclesiastical purposes.

Born in Northampton. Trained, Northampton
School of Art and Royal College of Art in book
illustration and wood engraving. Fellow,
Society of Designer-Craftsmen. Member, Art
Workers' Guild. Work in Victoria & Albert
Museum, Northampton Museum, Lincoln
Cathedral. Publications, *Design for Embroidery
from Traditional English Sources*, 1956;
Inspiration for Embroidery, 1966.

Sells direct to clients.

LAW Mary
40a Burlington Avenue, Kew Gardens, Surrey
tel: 01-878 1037
visitors by appointment

Various techniques – stool and chair covers,
cushions, rugs, wallhangings, stoles, wraps, bags.

Born in Kent. Trained, St Martins School of Art;
Central School of Art & Crafts. Member,
Society of Designer-Craftsmen. Exhibition:
1968, Ceylon Tea Centre, London.

Sells direct to clients and Le-Noy, London.

LEWIS Judith
Now living in Canada.
c/o Crafts Advisory Committee,
12 Waterloo Place, London SW1Y 4AU

Panels – themes based on landscapes, vivid
colours painted onto calico, variety of
embroidery techniques used.

Born in Wales. Trained, Manchester College of
Art & Design. Work in the collection of
Manchester Education Authority. Exhibitions:
1974, Park Square Gallery, Leeds; 1975,
Gallery 27, Tonbridge. Published three articles
in *Creative Crafts*, March, April, May, 1975.

Sells direct to clients.

LYON Mary
Greystone Cottage, Tyn-y-Groes, Conway,
Gwynedd LL32 8SZ, Wales
tel: 049 267 455
visitors by appointment

Patchwork – quilts, cushions, clothes.

Trained, Denman College. Exhibition: 1971,
Dolgellau, Wales.

Sells direct to clients.

MAXWELL Susan
Susans Cottage Industry,
7 Southwood Lawn Road, London N6
tel: 01-348 5485
visitors by appointment

Appliqué – wall hangings and bedspreads.

Born in South Africa. Trained, London College
of Printing as graphic designer and typographer.
Member, Society of Designer-Craftsmen.

Sells direct to clients and No Man's Hand,
London.

MURDOCH Sue
34 Pickets Street, Balham, London SW12 8QB
tel: 01-673 0010
visitors by appointment

Framed collage pictures and appliqué
bedspreads. Pictures are glued using fabrics,
braids, beads and sometimes paper. Bedspreads
are hand or machine stitched.

Published article in *Creative Crafts*, March, 1975.

Sells direct to clients.

PICK Mary
Cedar Lodge, Molly Hurst Lane, Woolley,
Nr Wakefield, West Yorkshire
tel: 022 678 2577
visitors by appointment

Canvas work and appliqué – cushions, hangings,
rugs, panels, hammocks, swings – dresses to
commission.

Trained Manchester College of Art;
Winchester School of Art. Member, 62 Group of
the Embroiderers' Guild; Society of Designer-
Craftsmen.

Sells direct to clients; Strangeways, London.

RISLEY Christine
16 Baizdon Road, Blackheath, London SE3
tel: 01-852 2533
no visitors

Machine embroidery – particularly interested in
writing and lecturing on machine embroidery,
historical and contemporary, covering all
aspects of domestic, trade and industrial machine
embroidery.

Born in England. Trained, Goldsmiths College.
Work in the collections of Carlisle, Coventry,
Derby, Essex, Fife, Hertford, Leicester,
Montgomery, Nottingham, Oxford, Reading,
Shropshire and Inner London Education
Committees and at Westminster College,
Oxford. Publications, *Machine Embroidery*, 1961;
Creative Embroidery, 1969; *Machine Embroidery: a
Complete Guide*, 1973. Teaches, Goldsmiths
College.

Sells direct to clients.

SIDA Glenys
3 Avon Road, Walthamstow, London E17
tel: 01-520 3314
visitors by appointment

Machine and hand stitched collage using fabrics –
pictorial representations of buildings and figures.

Born in Cheshire. Trained, St Martins School of
Art. Teaches, Joseph Clark School for Partially
Sighted Children.

Sells direct to clients.

WALTON Flora
3 Penshurst Walk, Bromley, Kent
tel: 01-460 8650
visitors by appointment

Decorative panels and ecclesiastical work using metal threads.

Trained, Goldsmiths College. Fellow, Society of Designer-Craftsmen. Work at Victoria & Albert Museum; Reading Art Gallery; in the collections of many Education Authorities and at Bishop Otter College. Exhibition: 1970, Ditchling Art Gallery.

Sells direct to clients.

WARREN Verina
Greystone Cottage, Bagshaw Hill, Bakewell, Derbyshire DE4 1DL
tel: 062 981 3201
visitors by appointment

Small decorative machine-embroidered panels combining painting, printing, spraying and hand couched gold threads.

Born in Durham. Trained, Goldsmiths College. Member, 62 Group of the Embroiderers' Guild. Exhibition: 1975, North West Arts Association, Manchester. Teaches, Manchester Polytechnic.

Sells direct to clients and at Yew Tree Cottage Gallery; Park Square Gallery; Oxford Gallery.

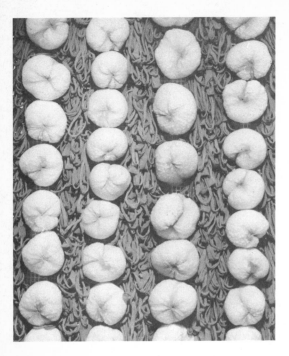

WILLIAMS Janice
Sheldon Cottage, The Bottoms, Epney, Saul,
Gloucestershire
tel: 045 274 639
visitors by appointment

Gold and metal thread embroidery, canvas work
and nylon and polystyrene hangings.

Trained, Royal School of Needlework.
Member, West of England Association of
Craftsmen. Work in the collection of
Leicestershire Education Committee. Teaches,
Gloucestershire College of Education;
Churchdown School; Dean Close School.

Sells direct to clients.

DMYTRENKO Rene
11 King Street South, Rochdale, Lancashire
visitors by appointment

Machine knitting – quilts, cushions,
wallhangings, clothes.

For illustration see *Textiles: embroidery.*

FASSETT Kaffe
62 Fordwych Road, London NW2
tel: 01-452 3786
visitors by appointment

Hand-knitted garments using a variety of yarns
in many subtle colours.

Born in California. Trained, The Museum of
Fine Arts School, Boston. Work in collection of
Royal Scottish Museum, Edinburgh; Temple
Newsam, Leeds. See *Crafts*, March/April 1975.
Teaches, Royal College of Art; Bristol
Polytechnic.

Sells direct to clients and Browns, London.

See *Textiles: embroidery.*

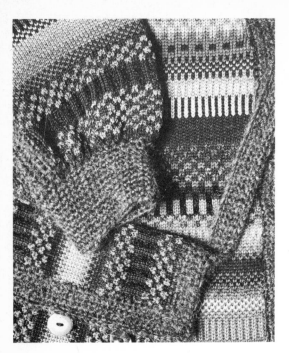

FEWLASS Anne
27 Tabley Road, London N7
visitors by appointment

Handknitting and domestic machine knitting.
Original knitwear for men and women using
mainly natural fibres such as wool, silk and
cotton; incorporating additional techniques and
materials including crochet, embroidery, beads
and leather.

Born in Yorkshire. Trained, Leicester College of
Art.

Sells direct to clients; Grey Flannel, London.

HINCHCLIFFE John
No 41, South Stoke, Nr Arundel, Sussex
tel: 0903 883103
visitors by appointment

Hand knitted garments in natural wool.

For illustration see *Textiles: weaving*.

HOLBOURNE David
New Haw Lock, Weybridge, Surrey
visitors by appointment

Machine knitting as a creative medium – dress
and furnishing fabrics, individual hangings and
sculptures – architectural commissions.

For illustration see *Textiles: weaving*.

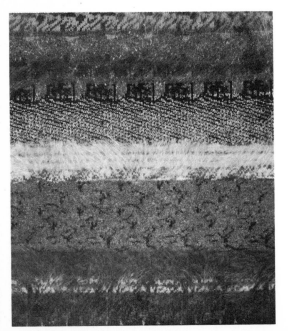

HUBBLE Virginia
Poldhurst Manor, Harbledown, Nr Canterbury,
Kent CT2 9AS
tel: 0227 66188
visitors by appointment

Machine and hand knitting. Yarns are natural
wools with small amounts of rayons, silks and
cotton to give varied colours and textures. Yarns
are hand-dyed to colours found in landscape;
inspiration for designs from sketches and
photographs of landscape. Clothes, panels, rugs,
cushions.

Born in Canterbury. Trained, Canterbury
College of Art; Winchester School of Art.
Teaches, Canterbury School of Art.

Sells Liberty, London; Fallowfields Gallery;
Bloomingdales.

KAGAN Sasha
The Llanerch, Llandinam, Powys
visitors by appointment

Hand knitting – dresses, capes, hangings,
bedspreads, garments – in pure wools.

Born in Hertfordshire. Trained, Exeter College
of Art & Design; Royal College of Art.
Teaches, Barnfield College, Luton.

Sells direct to clients and Browns, London;
Nam-Nam Skor; Betsy Bunky Bini.

KEMP Susan
Millbank Stables, Eyemouth,
Berwickshire TD14 5RE, Scotland
tel: 039 02 306
visitors by appointment

Machine knitting – designs for knitwear.

For illustration see *Textiles: batik and fabric
printing.*

MACKLAM Kay
8 Lower Caldecote, Biggleswade, Bedfordshire
tel: 0767 312452
visitors by appointment

Knitted fabrics made to order – for fashion and
interior design.

For illustration see *Textiles: weaving*.

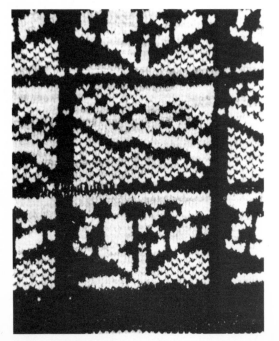

PEARSON Esther
51½ Stroud Green Road, London N4
tel: 01-263 1482
visitors by appointment

Machine knitting – fashion knitwear with
emphasis on fabric design and colour and use of
interesting yarn. Work is often hand dyed and
finished.

Born in London. Trained, Winchester School of
Art; Royal College of Art. Teaches,
Ravensbourne College of Art; Winchester
School of Art.

Sells direct to clients and Elle, London; Saks.

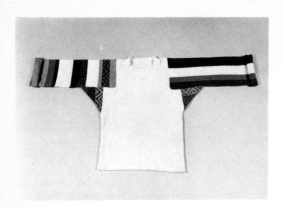

SHARIFI Pury
34 Coulston Road, Lancaster, Lancashire
tel: 0524 66973
visitors by appointment

Machine-knitted costumes, bedspreads, blankets
which are designed also to be used as
wallhangings, made from natural fibres,
hand-dyed.

Trained, Hornsey College of Art (Middlesex
Polytechnic).

Sells through Mirage, London; Folkcrafts.

SPARKES Brenda
Old Hall Farm, Main Street, East Leake
Loughborough, Leicestershire
tel: 050 982 2420
visitors by appointment

Wallhangings, rugs, cushions, clothes and
accessories using natural and man-made fibres.
Born in England. Trained, Loughborough
College of Art; Royal College of Art. Awarded
Workshipful Company of Weavers' Travel
Award, 1971. Teaches at Trent Polytechnic,
Nottingham.

Sells direct to clients.

See *Textiles: knitting and crochet*.

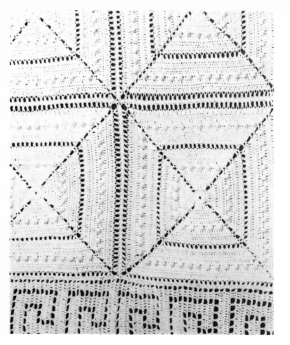

STRACHEY Mary
8 Pembroke Square, London w8 6pa
tel: 01–937 4974
visitors by appointment

Crocheted bedspreads in heavy cotton, white,
ivory, oatmeal – curtains and cushions to order.

Sells direct to clients and General Trading
Company; Boadicea; Colefax & Fowler,
London.

ABLETT Dorothy
Wantage House, 76 Dean Court Road,
Rottingdean, Sussex BN2 7DJ
tel: 0273 32530
visitors by appointment

Weaving for wallhangings and fashion – varied
designs, colours, sizes and techniques.

Born in Egypt. Trained, Kingston School of
Art; Central School of Art and Design; Chelsea
School of Art; Art Teacher's Diploma,
University of London; two year workshop
training with Ethel Mairet. Fellow, Society
of Designer-Craftsmen; Exhibiting Member,
Sussex Guild of Weavers; Bladon Gallery. Work
in collection of Contemporary Crafts,
Stoke-on-Trent Education Committee;
Teachers Training College, Hobart, Tasmania.
Exhibitions: 1968, The Grange, Rottingdean,
Sussex; 1971, Worthing Art Gallery.

Sells at the Peter Dingley Gallery and direct to
clients.

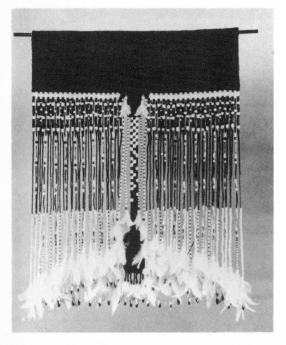

BAHOUTH Candace
Ebenezer Chapel, Pilton, Somerset
tel: 074 989 433
visitors by appointment

Individually designed woven hangings, fabrics,
body weavings – using tinsel, flashing lights,
feathers, glass, bells and beads.

Born in America. Trained, Syracuse University,
New York; one-year workshop training at The
Dove Centre, Somerset.

Sells direct to clients.

BARKER Mary
South Wing, One Harrington Road,
Brighton BN1 6RE
tel: 0273 551840
visitors by appointment

Woven wallhangings, cushions and small items
such as hairbands and necklets.

Trained, Leeds University; Art Teacher's
Diploma Course at Hornsey College of Art.
Member, Society of Designer-Craftsmen.
Exhibitions: 1971, The Grange, Rottingdean,
Sussex; 1972, travelling exhibition in Australia;
Robert MacDougal Art Gallery, New Zealand;
War Memorial Museum, New Zealand; 1974,
University of British Columbia, Vancouver,
Canada.

Sells direct to clients.

BEUTLICH Tadek
Club Fustera, La Fustera, Benisa, Alicante,
Spain
visitors by appointment

Woven wallhangings, heavily textured.

BRENNAN Archie
Edinburgh Tapestry Co, Dovecot Road,
Edinburgh 12
tel: 031 334 4118
visitors by appointment

Tapestry, wallhangings and constructions.

Born near Edinburgh. Trained, Edinburgh
College of Art; as apprentice at Edinburgh
Tapestry (Dovecot Studios) and Golden Targe
Studio, Edinburgh. Awarded Creative Arts
Fellowship, Australian National University,
1975; 1st Major Art Award, Scottish Arts
Council, 1974. Member, Society of Scottish
Artists; International Institute of Conservation.
Work in Aberdeen Art Gallery; Scottish Arts
Council; Royal Scottish Museum, Edinburgh.
Exhibitions: 1972, Scottish Arts Council; 1973,
Gallery 57, Edinburgh; 1974, Aberdeen Art
Gallery. Teaches, Edinburgh College of Art.

Sells direct to clients.

BUXTON Joanna
401½ Workshops, 401½ Wandsworth Road,
London sw8 2JP
tel: 01-622 7261/2
visitors by appointment

Highloom traditionally woven tapestries, using
wool, cotton or any materials suitable to
subject. Figurative, realistic subjects.

Born in Hertfordshire. Trained, Hornsey
College of Art and Royal College of Art. Series
of three tapestries with ballooning theme for
Gatwick Airport; two tapestries of games for
Central Electricity Generating Board.

Sells direct to public.

CADY Anna
CALA, 27 Warkworth Street, Cambridge
tel: 0223 65802
visitors by appointment

Fine materials in natural fibres, including silk, for clothing. Wallhangings, weaving and batik using natural dyes. Some upholstery materials. Materials woven on Swedish countermarch loom. Experimenting with natural dyes using natural yarns.

For illustration see *Textiles: batik and fabric printing.*

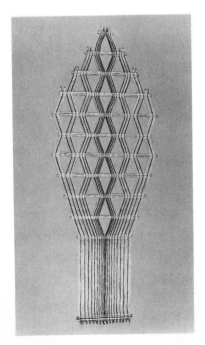

COLLINGWOOD Peter
Old School, Nayland, Colchester CO6 4JH
tel: 0206 262401
visitors by appointment

Floor rugs (both flat and pile) and wallhangings; macrogauzes, comprised of thin metal rods strung together to form ziggurats in two and three dimensions.

Born in London. Qualified as doctor; trained in workshops of Ethel Mairet, Barbara Sawyer and Alastair Morton. Awarded Gold Medal at International Handicrafts Exhibition, Munich, 1963; Awarded bursary from CAC 1974; OBE 1974. Member, Society of Designer-Craftsmen; Weavers Workshop; Suffolk Guild of Craftsmen. Travelling exhibition in USA: 1971, Three British Weavers; other exhibitions: 1974, Lantern Gallery, Michigan; 1974, Ashgate Gallery; 1975, Kunstindustrimuseum, Oslo and Copenhagen; Oxford Gallery. Publications, *Technique of Rug Weaving; Technique of Sprang; Peter Collingwood – His Weaves and Weaving.* Teaches in USA about one month a year.

Sells direct to public; Peter Dingley; Arras.

COX Bobbie
Warren House, Dartington, Totnes, Devon
tel: 0803 863132
visitors by appointment

Woven hangings and tapestry in wool processed from raw fleece, woven on purpose made frames to suit scale of work up to 6 feet by 8 feet.

Born in Norfolk. Trained, Bath Academy of Art. Member, Devon Guild of Craftsmen. Work in collections of South West Arts, Victoria & Albert Museum. Exhibitions: 1972, Exeter University Gallery; 1972, Guildford House, Surrey.

Sells direct to public.

DAGLISH Peter and Marian
13 Esmond Road, Chiswick, London w4
tel: 01-995 1293
visitors by appointment

Wallhangings in wool, punchwork.

Born in England. Trained, Ecole des Beaux-Arts, Montreal; Slade School of Fine Art. Work in University of Victoria, Canada; The Canada Council, Ottawa, Canada. Exhibitions: 1971, The Nita Forrest Gallery, Victoria, Canada; 1972-1973, Acadia University; New Brunswick Museum; Centennial Art Gallery; University of New Brunswick, Memorial University Art Gallery; 1974, Oxford Gallery, Bear Lane Gallery, Oxford; Canada House Gallery, London, Centre Culturel Canadien, Paris. Teach, The Slade School of Fine Art; Chelsea School of Art.

Sell direct to clients.

EPHSON Penelope

401½ Workshops, 401½ Wandsworth Road,
London SW8 2JP
tel: 01-622 7261/2
visitors by appointment

Weaves material suitable for furnishings and
garments and makes completed items such as
cushions, wallhangings, bedspreads, floor rugs,
shawls and scarves. Yarn is usually hand-dyed
wool but also uses silk and other yarns.

Born in London. Trained, Canterbury College
of Art; West Surrey College of Art and Design.
Licientiate of the Society of Designer-
Craftsmen.

Sells direct to clients; Liberty, Medina, London;
Harris Centre.

GARWOOD-YOUNG Karen

Reed Cottage, Staple, Nr Canterbury,
Kent CT3 1JZ
tel: 030 481 812625
visitors by appointment

Individually designed Rya rugs mostly made of
wool and flax.

Trained, West Sussex College of Art and Crafts,
also in Lancashire Mills; won RSA Bursary 1958
and studied in Scandinavia. Member, Royal
Society of Arts.

Sells direct to public; works to commission only.

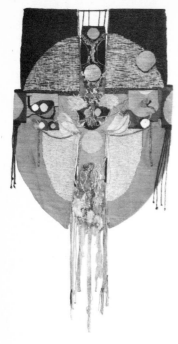

GILBY Myriam
82 Princes Road, Buckhurst Hill, Essex
tel: 01-505 6195
visitors evenings and weekends by appointment

Woven hangings employing some tapestry
techniques, but using many other individual
techniques, eg braiding, macramé, binding,
finger weaving, extra warps, to give a three-
dimensional effect. Designs are non-figurative.

Trained with Ruth Hurle. Member, Society of
Designer-Craftsmen; Association of Guilds of
Weavers, Spinners & Dyers. Exhibitions: 1968,
The Trinity Galleries, Colchester; 1970,
B H Corner Gallery, London. Work at St
Martin's College, Lancaster; in collection of
Gloucestershire County Council. Publication,
Free Weaving, London, 1975. Teaches,
Luton Girls School, Essex.

Sells direct to clients and Sheila David Gallery,
London.

HARRIS Ruth
George's Farm, Wimbish, Saffron Walden,
Essex
tel: 079 987 342
visitors by appointment

Tapestry.

Trained and teaches at Central School of Art &
Crafts. Work in Victoria & Albert Museum
and private collections in Britain and the
United States.

Sells direct to clients.

HAY-EDIE Gerd
84 Old Killowen Road, Rostrevor, Newry,
N. Ireland
tel: 069 373 373
visitors by appointment

Irish tweeds for fashion and furnishings –
curtains, wallhangings.

Born in Norway. Trained, Statens Kvinnelige
Industri-Skole, Oslo, Norway. Fellow, Society
of Industrial Artists and Designers.

Sells direct to clients.

HEIKKILA Pirkko
33 Albion Street, Rotherhithe, London SE16
tel: 01-237 1261 or 01-237 4668
visitors by appointment

Wallhangings and other articles.

Trained at a weaving school in Finland; The
Camberwell School of Arts with Tadek
Beutlich. Member, London Guild of Weavers;
The Handweavers & Spinners Guild in
Australia.

Sells direct to public and Sheila David Gallery,
London.

HERNMARCK Helena
392 West Broadway, New York, NY 10012, USA
tel: 212 966 7144
visitors by appointment

Large tapestries usually made of wool, sometimes using plastics – designs are abstract or photographic.

Born in Stockholm. Trained, Swedish State School for Art, Craft and Design, Stockholm. Awarded the American Institute of Architects', Craftsmanship Medal, 1973. Work in Los Angeles County Museum of Art; Museum of Modern Art, New York; National Gallery of Victoria, Melbourne; National Museum, Stockholm. Exhibitions: 1973, Museum of Modern Art, New York; 1974, Los Angeles County Museum of Art.

Sells direct to clients.

HILL David
11A Westwood Hill, Sydenham, London SE26
tel: 01-778 7776
visitors by appointment

Woven wallhangings, rugs, textile sculptures.

Trained, Camberwell School of Art and Crafts. Teaches, Camberwell School of Art & Crafts; Lanchester Polytechnic.

Sells direct to clients.

HINCHCLIFFE John
No 41, South Stoke, Nr Arundel, Sussex
tel: 0903 883103
visitors by appointment

Wallhangings or rugs, both very large and small.
Made from wide range of materials from rags to
handspun wools, his latest work is mostly pile-
woven rag rugs.

Trained, West Sussex College of Art;
Camberwell School of Art & Crafts;
Konstfackskolan Stockholm; Royal College of
Art. Teaches, Camberwell School of Art; West
Sussex College of Art.

Accepts commissions from the public and from
architects.

See *Textiles: knitting and crochet.*

HODGE Maureen
16 Hugh Miller Place, Edinburgh 3, Scotland
tel: 031 229 4472 Ex 68 (day)
031 332 8272 (evenings)
visitors by appointment

Individual hangings, sometimes three-
dimensional.

Trained, Edinburgh College of Art; awarded
Andrew Grant Post-Graduate Scholarship.
Member, Society of Scottish Artists. Work in
collections of Scottish Arts Council; Royal
Scottish Museum, Edinburgh; Stirling
University. Teaches, Edinburgh College of Art.

Sells direct to public and takes commissions.

HOLBOURNE David
New Haw Lock, Weybridge, Surrey
visitors by appointment

Dress and furnishing fabrics, individual hangings and sculptures architectural commissions.

Trained, St Martin's School of Art; Camberwell School of Art; studied under Tadek Beutlich. Teaches, Kingston Polytechnic; Winchester School of Art.

Sells direct to clients.

See *Textiles: knitting and crochet.*

LYKKEN Berit
Halsdon, Dolton, Nr Winkleigh, Devon
tel: 080 54 214
visitors by appointment

Large wallhangings, using mainly wool – simplified, goemetrical shapes of human figures and animals.

Born in Norway. Trained, The State College of Arts and Crafts, Oslo, Norway; Central School of Art and Design; one and a half years weaving training at Ravensbourne College of Art and Hammersmith College of Art. Member of Young Artists Association, Oslo.

Sells direct to clients.

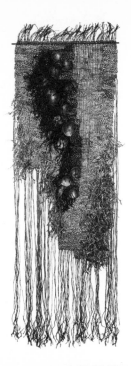

MABON Robert
Tanglewood, Wilton Lane, Jordans
Beaconsfield, Buckinghamshire HP9 2RG
tel: 024 07 3189
visitors by appointment

Rugs in double-weave technique using wool
and horsehair – tapestries and hangings using
various techniques and yarns with the emphasis
on contrast of material and texture.

Born in Durham. Trained, Camberwell School
of Art and Crafts; Central School of Art and
Design. Associate Member of Craftsmen Potters
Association; Associate Member of Devon Guild
of Craftsmen. Exhibitions: 1968, British Craft
Centre; 1969, Peter Dingley Gallery, Stratford
on Avon; 1972, Salix, Windsor; 1973, Chagford
Gallery, Devon.

Sells direct to clients; Boadicea London;
Chagford Gallery; Peter Dingley Gallery;
Craftwork; Salix.

See *Pottery*.

MACKLAM Kay
8 Lower Caldecote, Biggleswade
Bedfordshire
tel: 0767 312452
visitors by appointment

Hand woven furnishing fabrics, warp printed;
also knitted fabrics.

Trained at Goldsmiths College School of Art.
Teaches at St Martin's College of Art.

Sells direct to public.

See *Textiles: knitting and crochet*.

McFARLANE Kathleen
The Croft, Stody
Nr Melton Constable, Norfolk
tel: 026 386 505
visitors by appointment

Woven three-dimensional tapestries, mainly in sisal.

Work in St Margaret's Priory, Norfolk. Exhibitions: 1973, Weavers Workshop, Edinburgh; 1974, Sunderland Civic Art Gallery; 1976, British Crafts Centre.

Sells direct to clients; Casson Gallery, Sheila David Gallery, London; Norwich Castle Museum Craft Shop; Oxford Gallery.

McNEILL Mary
32 Parkstone Avenue, Southsea
Hampshire PO4 0QZ
tel: 0705 31075
visitors by appointment

Wallhangings and furnishing fabrics; dress-lengths, shawls and bags, handwoven in a variety of yarns.

Member of Society of Designer-Craftsmen. Work in the collection of Reading Museum.

Sells direct to the public.

MITCHELL Alison
26 King Henry's Road, London, NW3
tel: 01-586 2729
visitors by appointment

Two and three-dimensional functional objects, such as floor cushions, rugs, room dividers, all highly decorated.

Born in Oxford. Trained at Cambridge College of Art; Loughborough College of Art and Design; Camberwell College of Art and Crafts. Teaches at Ravensbourne College of Art.

Sells on commission from workshop.

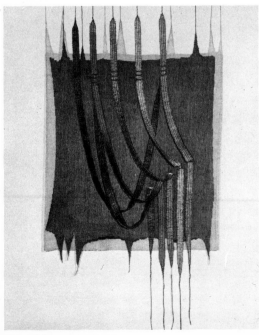

MOORMAN Theo
Stonebarrow, Painswick
Gloucestershire GL6 6YA
tel: 0452 2035
visitors by appointment

Ecclesiastical textiles woven in inlay technique using a variety of materials – wallhangings on a domestic scale woven in fine linen and cotton yarns.

Born in Yorkshire. Trained, Central School of Art and Crafts. Member of Art Workers Guild; Guild of Gloucestershire Craftsmen. Work in Royal Northern College of Music; Cooper Hewit Museum, New York; Manchester Cathedral; Gloucester Cathedral; Ripon Cathedral; Whitelands College, Putney; St Mary's College, Cheltenham. Exhibitions: 1971, Arts and Crafts Society Gallery, Oregon, Arts Society Gallery, California; 1972, Academy of Arts, Honolulu; 1975, Oxford Gallery, Royal Northern College of Music.

Sells direct to clients.

MORGAN Fay
2 School Cottages, Wellington Heath
Ledbury, Hereford & Worcester HR8 ILU
tel: 0531 2718
visitors by appointment

Fabrics designed in relation to garment shape
and purpose, incorporating hand stitching and
finishing.

Born in Wales. Trained, Hornsey College of
Art; Royal College of Art. Awarded Welsh
Arts Council/Crafts Advisory Committee
Bursary 1975/76. Member of Society of
Designer-Craftsmen. Publications, *Clothes
Without Patterns*, Mills and Boon, 1976. Teaches
at Goldsmiths College.

Sells direct to clients; Collection, London.

MULLINS Barbara
Graffham Weavers, Petworth, Sussex
tel: 079 86 348
visitors by appointment

Bedspreads, cushions, bags, cloth and rugs in
natural dyed wools.

Member of Society of Designer-Craftsmen.
Work in collection of Worcester Cathedral;
Trinity College, Oxford. Exhibitions: 1965,
Ceylon Tea Centre; 1967 and 1969, Edinburgh;
1970, British Craft Centre; 1972, Craftwork,
Guildford. Teaches at West Dean College,
Chichester; Graffham Weavers.

Sells direct to clients; Craftwork.

MULLINS Gwen
Graffham Weavers, Petworth, Sussex
tel: 079 86 260
visitors by appointment

Floor-rugs, bedspreads, cushions and cloth made from natural dyed wools.

Born in London. Member of London Guild of Weavers, Spinners and Dyers; Society of Designer-Craftsmen. Work in collection of Victoria & Albert Museum; Worcester Cathedral. Exhibitions: 1965, Ceylon Tea Centre; 1967 and 1969 Edinburgh; 1970, British Craft Centre; 1972, Craftwork, Guildford.

Sells direct to clients; Craftwork.

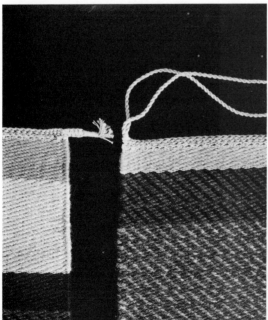

OATES Roger
2 School Cottages, Wellington Heath, Ledbury
Hereford & Worcester, HR8 1LU
tel: 0531 2718
visitors by appointment

Woven rugs and carpets in clear colours for floors and walls – specially co-ordinated interior projects.

Born in Yorkshire. Trained, York School of Art; West Surrey College of Art and Design. Member of Worcestershire Guild of Weavers. Work in collection of Reading Museum and Art Gallery; Morley College, London; Malvern Hills College; Australian Council for the Arts. Teaches at Winchester School of Art.

Sells direct to clients; Collection, London.

RIEGLER Maggie
Dess Station, Kincardine O'Neil
Aberdeenshire, Scotland
tel: 033 984 254
visitors by appointment

Two- and three-dimensional hangings,
incorporating macramé, plaiting and braiding,
using a variety of materials.

Trained, Gray's School of Art, Aberdeen.
Member of Weaver's Workshop, Edinburgh.
Exhibition: 1969, Civic Arts Centre, Aberdeen.
Teaches at Gray's School of Art, Aberdeen.

Sells direct to clients.

ROBERTSON Vanessa
Chy-an-Gwyador, Bojewyan Stennack
Pendeen, Penzance, Cornwall, TR19 7TR
visitors by appointment

Floor rugs, wallhangings, large cushions, bags
and clothes woven in natural linen, cotton and
wool yarns and woollen rags.

Born in Cambridge. Member of Devon Guild of
Craftsmen; Cornwall Crafts Association. Works
in partnership with Norman Young.

Sells direct to clients; Craftwork; Oxford
Gallery; Coexistence; Barbican Craft Market;
Bristol Guild of Applied Arts; Folkcrafts.

SLATER Heather
195 Rosendale Road, London SE21 8LW
tel: 01-670 8787
visitors by appointment

Rugs and wallhangings, functional items, soft toys –renovating and/or redressing antique dolls.

Trained, Camberwell School of Arts and Crafts; Goldsmith's College, School of Art.

Sells direct to clients.

SMITTEN Margaret
Flat 12, Digswell House, Monks Rise
Welwyn Garden City, Hertfordshire
tel: 96 21117
visitors by appointment

Wallhangings and panels – often based on the layouts of formal gardens and country estates.

Born in Hertford. Trained, Brighton Polytechnic. Fellow and Member of Executive Committee of the Digswell Arts Trust; Associate Member of the West Herts Guild of Weavers, Spinners and Dyers; Member of the 62 Group of the Embroiderers' Guild. Exhibition: 1975, Mariposa, St Albans. Teaches at Hitchin College.

Sells direct to clients; Digswell Gallery.

See *Toys and puppets*.

SPARKES Brenda
Old Hall Farm, Main Street, East Leake
Loughborough, Leicestershire
tel: 050 982 2420
visitors by appointment

Wallhangings, rugs, cushions, clothes and
accessories using natural and man-made fibres.
Born in England. Trained, Loughborough
College of Art; Royal College of Art. Awarded
Workshipful Company of Weavers' Travel
Award, 1971. Teaches at Trent Polytechnic,
Nottingham.

Sells direct to clients.

See *Textiles: knitting and crochet*.

SPOONER Susan
The Old Farmhouse, Little Trebarveth Foundry
Stithians, Cornwall
visitors by appointment

Simply shaped coats and garments incorporating
tapestry, landscapes; wallhangings in wool and
cotton.

Born in Cheshire. Trained, Cardiff College of
Art; Goldsmiths College, School of Art.
Awarded Crafts Advisory Committee New
Craftsmen's Grant, 1975. Member of Cornwall
Crafts Association; Cornwall Guild of Weavers,
Spinners and Dyers. Work in collection of
Truro Cathedral.

Sells direct to clients.

SQUIRE Colin
Sheldon Cottage, The Bottoms, Epney, Saul
Gloucestershire GL2 7LN
tel: 045 274 639
visitors by appointment

Rugs and cushions in linen and wool,
wallhangings using mainly geometric designs in
fine linen – textile constructions using nylon
monofilament on perspex.

Born in Middlesex. Trained, Camberwell
School of Arts and Crafts; University of Leeds.
Member of West of England Association of
Craftsmen.

Sells direct to clients; Peter Dingley.

SUTTON Ann
Farnborough Barn, Farnborough,
Nr Banbury, Oxfordshire OX17 1EG
tel: 029 589 678
visitors by appointment

Two- and three-dimensional hangings and
objects.

Born in Staffordshire. Trained, Cardiff College
of Art. Commission Award from Welsh Arts
Council for sculpture, 1970; Travel Award from
Workshipful Company of Weavers, 1971.
Fellow of the Society of Industrial Artists and
Designers; Fellow of the Royal Society of Arts.
Work in collection of Victoria & Albert
Museum; New Law Courts, Cheshire; National
Museum of Wales, Cardiff; CAC collection.
Exhibitions: 1969, British Crafts Centre; 1970,
Victoria and Albert Museum travelling
exhibition. Teaches at North Oxon Technical
College, Banbury and annually at Glamorgan
Summer School.

Sells direct to clients.

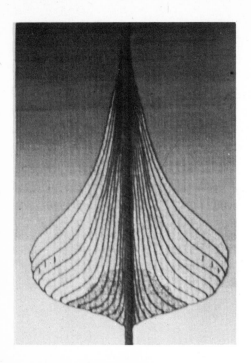

TAYLOR Roderick
Ponden Hall, Stanbury, Near Haworth
West Yorkshire
tel: 0535 44154
visitors by appointment

Clothes, wallhangings, rugs; fabrics and shawls
using natural fibres.

Member of Guild of Yorkshire Craftsmen;
Lakeland Guild of Craftsmen; Bladon Gallery.
Work in St John's College, Oxford.
Exhibitions: 1975, Yorkshire Show,
Harrogate.

Sells direct to clients.

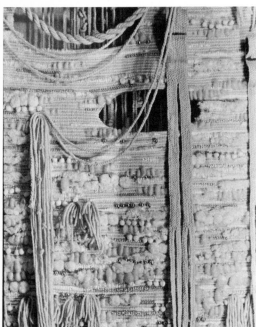

WALLER Irene
249 Hagley Road, Edgbaston, Birmingham
visitors by appointment

Wall and space hangings using mixed textile
and other techniques.

Born in Birmingham. Trained, Birmingham
College of Art. Awarded Royal Society of Arts
Travelling Scholarship, 1969. Fellow, Royal
Society of Arts; Associate of Royal Birmingham
Society of Artists; Member, Guild of Weavers
and Spinners. Work in Dudley College of
Education; Halesowen Parish Church; St Anne'
Church, Moseley; Church of England Chapel,
Stoneleigh. Exhibitions: 1970, Alexandra
Theatre, Birmingham; 1971, New Art Gallery,
Birmingham; Midlands Art Centre; Lazarus
Store Gallery, Ohio; McCurdy's Store Gallery,
New York; 1972, New Art Gallery,
Birmingham; Shaw-Rimmington Gallery.
New York; 1974, Foyles Bookshop; 1975,
Weald Publishing Company, Tunbridge Wells

Sells direct to clients.

WIJEWARDENE Anoma
11 Onslow Court, Drayton Gardens
London SW10
tel: 01-373 3028
visitors by appointment

Fabrics woven and hand-painted for dress and
interior, using silk in conjunction with various
fibres – work ranges from jackets, scarves and
bags to wallhangings, cushions and quilts.

Born in Sri Lanka. Trained at Central School of
Art and Crafts. Member of Society of Designer-
Craftsmen. Exhibition: 1973, Sekers, Sloane
Street.

Sells direct to clients: Libertys; Elle; Feathers;
Parker's; Lucienne Phillips; Zarach, London;
Serge Guilloux.

BLYTH Jane
76 West Street, Farnham, Surrey
tel: 025 13 5559
visitors by appointment

Wooden constructions – houses, beds, boats, with peg doll inmates.

Born in Surrey.

Sells direct to clients and Craftwork.

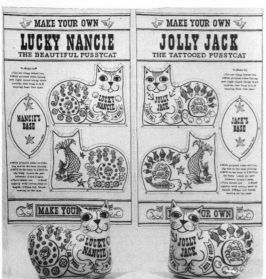

ELLIOTT Louise
Bridgers Farmhouse, Hurstpierpoint, Sussex
tel: 0273 832716
visitors by appointment

Design of rag toys – dolls, animals and birds – printed on cloth ready for making-up.

Trained at Brighton College of Art.

Sells direct to clients.

FULLER Ronald
Laxfield, Woodbridge, Suffolk IP13 8DX
tel: 098 683 317
visitors by appointment

Wooden toy aeroplanes, ships, submarines –
replica Victorian toys – electronic and
clockwork toys – hot-air balloons and kites.

Born in Cornwall. Trained, Falmouth School of
Art; Royal College of Art.

Sells direct to clients and Heals, Pollocks Toy
Museum, Owl & Pussycat, London; Friars
Gallery, Edward Bull, Plega, Leigh Gallery.

SMITTEN Margaret
Flat 12, Digswell House, Monks Rise
Welwyn Garden City, Hertfordshire
tel: 96 21117
visitors by appointment

Dolls – machine embroidered or screenprinted.

For illustration see *Textiles: weaving*.

WRIGHT John
14 Dagmar Passage, London N1 2DN
tel: 01-226 1787
visitors by appointment

Marionettes carved in wood – sometimes other types of puppets.

Born in South Africa. Trained, School of Applied Art, Capetown. Awarded CAC bursary 1974. Member of International Union of Puppeteers. Publication, *Your Puppetry*, Sylvan Press, London, 1951.

Sells direct to clients.

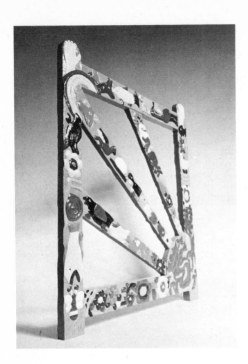

PAKENHAM-WALSH Mabel
12 Speke Road, St Peters, Nr Broadstairs
Isle of Thanet, Kent
tel: 0843 65273
visitors by appointment

Wood, carved and painted to form decorative panels.

Born in Lancashire. Trained at Lancaster College of Art. Exhibitions: 1963, Collectors' Gallery, Portobello Road; 1968, Santa Barbara Public Library; 1971, Langton Gallery, World's End, Chelsea.

Sells direct to clients.

PYE David
Regency House Downgate, Tidebrook
Wadhurst, Sussex
tel: 089 288 3110
visitors by appointment

Wood carving – from lettering to figureheads, particularly bowls and dishes. Wood turning – boxes, some carved as well as turned. Also wood sculpture and restoration of carving on antique furniture and buildings.

Member, Architectural Association; Royal Institute of British Architects; Society of Industrial Artists and Designers. Work in Victoria and Albert Museum. Publications *Ships*, Penguin, London 1948; *Nature of Design*, Studio Vista, London 1964; *The Nature and art of workmanship*, Cambridge University Press 1968.

Sells direct to clients.

RAFFAN Richard
Great Uppacott, Tedburn St Mary
Exeter EX6 6DN
tel: 064 76 578
visitors by appointment

Turned bowls, platters, scoops and boxes in
English and foreign hardwoods.

Trained for a short time with Douglas Hart at
Dartington.

Sells direct to clients; Heals, Casson Gallery,
David Mellor, London; Seasons.

SHAVE Alan
Dunloe, Peppard, Henley-on-Thames
Oxon RG9 5HD
tel: 073 525 3142
no visitors

Wood turning – domestic ware in various
woods – bowls, platters.

Born in Middlesex. Trained, Hammersmith
College of Arts & Building.

Sells direct to clients.

SMITH Sam
The Golf House, Kingswear, Dartmouth
Devon TQ6 0DZ
tel: 080 425 360
visitors by appointment

Wood carved and painted – boats, animals,
figures – humorous and satirical comments on
life.

Born in Hampshire. Trained at art school in
London. Work in City Art Gallery, Bristol.
Exhibition, 1972, City Art Gallery, Bristol;
Beaford Art Centre; Camden Art Centre,
London.

Sells direct to clients.

BARNSLEY Edward
Cockshott Lane, Stoner Hill, Froxfield
Petersfield, Hampshire
tel: 073 084 233
visitors by appointment

Individual domestic, college, church, cathedral
and business furniture.

Born in Gloucestershire. Member of the Society
of Designer-Craftsmen; Art Workers' Guild.
Work in Melbourne Art Gallery; at the House of
Lords and in Canterbury Cathedral.

Sells direct to clients.

GRIERSON Martin
5 Dryden Street, London WC2E 9NW
tel: 01-240 2430
visitors by appointment

Individual furniture, mainly to commission, in
high quality wood and selected veneers.

Born in London. Trained Central School of Art
& Crafts. Fellow of the Society of Industrial
Artists and Designers. Teaches, Central School
of Art & Design and High Wycombe College
of Art & Design.

Sells direct to clients.

HOYTE Peter
Millbridge, Frensham, Nr Farnham, Surrey
tel: 025 125 3373
visitors by appointment

Design of furniture for production, particularly chairs and stools.

Sells direct to clients.

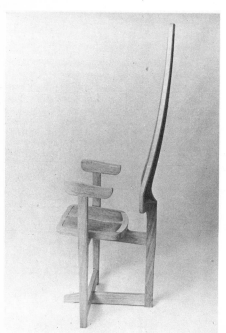

LA TROBE BATEMAN Richard
23 Ceylon Road, London W14 POY
tel: 01-603 4895
visitors by appointment

Chairs, tables, cabinets, screens in timber, cane and other traditional materials, using traditional techniques.

Born in London. Trained at St Martins School of Art and Royal College of Art. Teaches, St Martins School of Art.

Sells direct to clients and Bentalls.

LEACH Maurice
Henley Woodwork, Henley, Near Langport
Somerset TA10 9BH
tel: 0458 250750
visitors by appointment

Ladder-back chairs – dining, carver and
rocking – with rush seats. Also refectory tables,
panelled dressers and gate-leg tables. All in
English oak, ash or elm.

Born in London. Trained with F. Dukes & Son
and Y. J. Lovell, Sussex. Member of the
Somerset Guild of Craftsmen.

Sells direct to clients and Dartington Hall Shop.

MACKILLIGIN Sandy
The Hop Kiln, Puttenham, Guildford, Surrey
tel: 0483 81 0481
visitors by appointment

Individual furniture in a variety of woods –
mainly to commission.

Born in Hampshire. Trained, Beckenham School
of Art; in Edward Barnsley's workshop; in
Denmark. Teaches, West Surrey College of Art
& Design, Farnham; Brighton Polytechnic.

Sells direct to clients.

MAKEPEACE John
Farnborough Barn, Farnborough, Nr Banbury
Oxfordshire OX17 IEG
tel: 029 589 678
visitors by appointment

Design and execution of individual pieces and
groups of furniture for complete interiors –
simple forms, extensive range of materials.

Born in Warwickshire. Workshop training,
followed by periods of design study in
Scandinavia and North America. Fellow of the
Society of Industrial Artists and Designers,
Fellow of the Society of Designer-Craftsmen.
Exhibition: 1972, British Crafts Centre.
Contributed article to M. Schofield (ed.)
Decorative Art and Modern Interiors, Studio Vista,
London, 1975/76.

Sells Libertys London; Coexistence; Collection.

PETERS Alan
Aller Studio, Kentisbeare, Cullompton, Devon
tel: 088 46 251
visitors by appointment

Mainly commissioned work, single items or
complete room schemes – also smaller items
suitable for presentation.

Trained in workshop of Edward Barnsley;
Shoreditch College; Central School of Art &
Crafts. Awarded CAC bursary 1975. Member
of Society of Designer-Craftsmen.

Sells direct to clients.

PLUNKETT William
Redsan Works, 14/40 Sanderstead Road
South Croydon, Surrey
tel: 01-680 3571
visitors by appointment

Special projects for architects in aluminium
alloy and steel. Sculpture mainly in stainless and
mild steel for interiors and private collections.

Trained Kingston College of Art. Fellow of the
Society of Industrial Artists and Designers;
Fellow of the Royal Society of Arts. Work in
Victoria & Albert Museum.

Sells direct to clients.

SNEED George
Bacon's Barn, St Michael South Elmham
Bungay, Suffolk NR35 1NF
tel: 098 682 282
visitors by appointment

Furniture in various timbers, sometimes using
rush and plastics – mainly to commission. Also
small woodware.

Trained, Chelmsford School of Art; Shoreditch
College of Education. Fellow of the Society of
Designer-Craftsmen.

Sells direct to clients and Oxford Gallery.

AFFINITY
85 Golders Green Road, NW11
tel: 01-458 2962

AMALGAM
3 Barnes High Street, SW13
tel: 01-878 1279

ANGELA FLOWERS
3-4 Portland Mews,
D'Arblay Street, W1
tel: 01-734 0240

ANVIL
89 Dulwich Village, SE21
tel: 01-693 7733

AGENTA
84 Fulham Road, SW3
tel: 01-584 3119

ASSET GALLERY
Harvey Nichols,
78 Knightsbridge, SW3

ASPREY
165 New Bond Street, W1
tel: 01-493 6767

ATMOSPHERE
148 Regents Park Road, NW1
tel: 01-722 6058

BAYSWATER ROAD MARKET
W2
a street market

BERTRAM ROTA
4 Savile Row, W1
tel: 01-734 3860

BEST OF BRITISH
25 Museum Street, WC1
tel: 01-580 6285

BLADES
8 Burlington Gardens,
Savile Row, W1

BOADICEA
19 Beauchamp Place, SW3
tel: 01-584 2682

BOOTY JEWELLERY
9a New Bond Street, W1
tel: 01-629 6796

BRITISH CRAFTS CENTRE
43 Earlham Street, WC2
tel: 01-836 6993

BROWNS
25/27 South Molton Street, W1

CAMEO CORNER
26 Museum Street, WC1
tel: 01-637 0981

CASSON GALLERY
73 Marylebone High Street, W1
tel: 01-487 5080

CATHERINE BUCKLEY LTD
302 Westbourne Grove, W11

CENTAUR GALLERY
82 Highgate High Street, N6
tel: 01-340 0087

CHELSEA GLASSWORKS
105 Fulham Road, SW3
tel: 01-581 2501

CHIC OF HAMPSTEAD
Heath Street, NW3
tel: 01-435 5454

COLEFAX & FOWLER
39 Brook Street, W1

COLLINGWOOD
46 Conduit Street, W1
tel: 01-734 2111

CRAFT SHOP V & A
Victoria and Albert Museum,
South Kensington, SW7
tel: 01-589 5070

CRAFTSMEN POTTERS SHOP
Marshall Street, W1
tel: 01-437 7605

DUNHILL LTD
30 Duke Street, St James's, SW1
tel: 01-493 9161

ELECTRUM GALLERY
21 South Molton Street, W1
tel: 01-629 6325

ELLE
27 Sloane Square, SW1 and
12 New Bond Street, W1

FEATHERS
43 Kensington High Street, W8
tel: 01-937 2267
and New Bond Street, W1,
Hans Crescent, SW3

FORTNUM & MASON LTD
181 Piccadilly, W1
tel: 01-734 8040

FOYLES
Charing Cross Road, WC2

GARRARDS
112 Regents Street, W1

GENERAL TRADING COMPANY
144 Sloane Street, SW1
tel: 01-730 0411

THE GLASSHOUSE
27 Neal Street, WC2
tel: 01-836 9785

THE GREAT FROG
46A Carnaby Street, W1

GREY FLANNEL
7 Chiltern Street, W1

GROUP INTERIORS
19 High Street, Ealing, W5

HALCYON DAYS
14 Brook Street, W1

HARRODS
Knightsbridge, SW7

HATCHARDS
187 Piccadilly, W1

HEALS
196 Tottenham Court Road, W1
tel: 01-636 1666

HENNELL
1 Davies Street, W1
tel: 01-499 3011

HEYWOOD HILL
10 Curzon Street, W1

JOHN DONALD
10 The Square, Richmond,
Surrey

LE-NOY
58 Heath Street, Hampstead,
NW3

LIBERTY & CO
Regent Street, W1

LUCIENNE'S
69 Knightsbridge, SW7

MAGGS BROS.
50 Berkeley Square, W1
tel: 01-499 2007

MASON'S YARD GALLERY
6 Mason's Yard,
St. James's Street, SW1

MEDINA
10 West Halkin Street, W1

DAVID MELLOR
4 Sloane Square, SW1
tel: 01-730 4259

MIRAGE
6 Clarendon Cross, W11

MORLEY GALLERIES
4 Belmont Hill, Lewisham, SE1
tel: 01-852 6151

NEWSONS OF ENFIELD
Windmill Hill, Enfield
tel: 01-363 3675

NO MAN'S HAND
8 Spring Bridge Road,
Ealing Broadway
tel: 01-567 0529

THE OWL & THE PUSSYCAT
11 Flask Walk, Hampstead, NW3

PACIFIC 7
Market Place, W1
tel: 01-636 3516

PARROTS LTD
56 Fulham Road, SW3

PARKERS
13 Heath Street, Hampstead,
NW3

PISCES DESIGNS
5 Chiltern Street, W1

POLLOCKS TOY MUSEUM
1 Scala Street, W1
tel: 01-636 3452

PRESENTS
129 Sloane Street, SW1
tel: 01-730 5457

JOHN SANDOE LTD
10 Blacklands Terrace, SW3
tel: 01-589 9473

SEAN KELLY GALLERY
21 London Road, SE1
tel: 01-928 9722

SHEILA DAVID GALLERY
45 Chalcot Road, NW1
tel: 01-652 2581

STEVENS & CAPON
28 Lower Richmond Road,
SW15
tel: 01-789 8374

STRANGEWAYS
502 Kings Road, SW10
tel: 01-352 9863

THE TABLEWARE CENTRE
50 Burlington Arcade, W1
tel: 01-493 2151

TREADWELL GALLERY
36 Chiltern Street, W1
tel: 01-935 6739

TREASURE ISLAND
81 Pimlico Road, SW1
tel: 01-730 3630

TURRET BOOKSHOP
1B Kensington Church Walk,
W8
tel: 01-937 7583

TWENTY-FIRST CENTURY
58 Hill Rise, Richmond
tel: 01-948 2787

WARDROBE
17 and 42 Chiltern Street, W1
tel: 01-935 4086

ZARACH
183 Sloane Street, SW1

Shops and galleries outside London

ANDREE SAMSON
Paris, France

ARNOLFINI GALLERY
Narrow Quay, Bristol 1, Avon
tel: 0272 299191

ARRAS GALLERY
New York, USA

ART MART
Canterbury, Kent

ARTISAN
37 Penylan Road, Roath Park,
Cardiff, South Glamorgan
tel: 0222 30927

ATHENEA
Tunbridge Wells, Kent

BARBICAN CRAFT MARKET
The Harbour, Penzance,
Cornwall
tel: 0736 5610 or 5869

BARKERS OF LANERCOST
Holmefoot, Lanercost,
Brampton, Cumbria
tel: 06977 2638

BENTALLS
Kingston upon Thames, Surrey

BETSY BUNKY BINI
New York, USA

BIRMINGHAM ARTS SHOP
City Arcade, Birmingham

BLOOMINGDALES
New York, USA

BLUECOAT DISPLAY CENTRE
Bluecoat Chambers,
School Lane, Liverpool
tel: 051 709 4014

BOHUN GALLERY
Station Road,
Henley on Thames, Oxfordshire
tel: 049 12 6228

BOOKS AND CRAFTS
Brecon, Powys

BRAITHWAITE & DUNN
Nottingham

BRISTOL GUILD OF
APPLIED ART LTD
68–70 Park Street, Bristol
tel: 0272 25548

THE CERAMIC SHOP
Antwerp, Belgium

CHAGFORD GALLERIES
20 The Square, Chagford,
Devon
tel: 064 73 3287

CHAPEL GALLERIES
Wessex Craft Centre, High
Street, Tisbury, Wiltshire
tel: 074787 500

COB LANE CRAFT SHOP
Cob Lane, Tenby, Dyfed
tel: 0834 2775

COEXISTENCE
10 Argyle Street, Bath
tel: 0225 61507

COLLECTION
110 Hagley Road West,
Warley, West Midlands
tel: 021 429 8491

COPPER KETTLE
Much Hadam, Hertfordshire

CORNWALL CRAFTS
Middlebury, Vermont, USA

COUNTRY CRAFT
22 Market Street, Alton,
Hampshire
tel: 0420 85786

THE CRAFT CENTRE
Alstonfield, Derbyshire

THE CRAFT GALLERY
St Helier, Jersey

CRAFT HARVEST
Middle Street, Shere, Surrey
tel: 048 041 3167

CRAFT SHOP FLAMENT
Brussels, Belgium

CRAFTSMENS GALLERY
Woodstock, Oxfordshire

CRAFTWORK
38 Castle Street, Guildford
tel: 0483 77707

DARTINGTON HALL SHOP
Totnes, Devon

DAVID PAUL GALLERY
Chichester, Sussex

DEMBO OF BRISTOL
Bristol, Avon

THE DESIGN MINE
Old Bridge Street, Truro,
Cornwall
tel: 0872 77750

DIGSWELL GALLERY
Digswell House, Monks Rise,
Welwyn Garden City,
Hertfordshire
tel: 96 21506

DORCAS HARDIN
Washington, DC, USA

DOVE CRAFT SHOP & GALLERY
Dove Centre, Crispin Hall,
High Street, Street, Somerset
tel: 9924 5172

EDWARD BULL
Guildford, Surrey

EEF BORGER GALLERY
Utrecht, Netherlands

ELL SHOP
Dunkeld, Perthshire

EUROPEAN CRAFT CENTRE
Zurich, Switzerland

FALLOWFIELD GALLERY
Manchester

FIELD ART STUDIO
Berkeley, Michigan, USA

FOCUS GALLERY
108 Derby Road, Nottingham
tel: 0602 47913

FOLKCRAFTS
88 High Street, Totnes, Devon
tel: 0803 864207

FOREST BANK CRAFT SHOP
Taynuilt, Argyll

FORTY GALLERY
Horsham, Sussex

FORUM GALLERY
16 Market Street, Lanes,
Brighton, Sussex
tel: 0273 28578

FRAMERS GALLERY
Penzance, Cornwall

FRANK WALTON
Oban, Argyll

FRIARS GALLERY
Canterbury, Kent

GALERIE KÖSTER
Munich, Germany

GALERIE NOELLA GEST
San Rémy de Provence, France

GALLERY 10½
Hull, North Humberside

GALLERY 24
Shaftesbury, Dorset

GLOBAL VILLAGE CRAFTS
17 St James Street,
South Petherton, Somerset
tel: 0460 40194

GRANARY CRAFTS
Hurstpierpoint, Sussex

GREYFRIARS ART SHOP
Edinburgh

HANDMADE
The Cross, Calver, Nr Baslow,
Derbyshire
tel: 0433 3019

HARRIS CENTRE
Hawkhurst, Kent
tel: 05805 3315

HATTIE
Detroit, USA

HEALS
Guildford, Surrey

IAN CLARKSON GALLERY
West Bow, Edinburgh

INTERFORM
Brighton, Sussex

JOHN PIERCE
7 Lion Street, Rye, Sussex
tel: 079 73 3383

KANYA CRAFTS
Brighton, Sussex

KIMPTON CRAFTS AND ART
CENTRE
Kimpton, Hertfordshire
tel: 0438 932236 and 832235

LANTERN GALLERY
Manchester

LEIGH GALLERY
19 Kings Parade, Cambridge
tel: 0223 50303

LONGLEAT
Nr Warminster, Wiltshire

MALCOLM BISHOP
Manchester

MARIPOSA
Holywell Hill, St Albans,
Hertfordshire

MARY LOE
Nayland, West Suffolk

MEANDER
21 Elvet Bridge, Durham
tel: 0385 3553
also at Leeds and Newcastle

MINSTER
Coventry, Warwickshire

NAM-NAM SKOR
Stockholm, Sweden

NEW ASHGATE GALLERY
Wagon Yard, Downing Street,
Farnham, Surrey
tel: 025 13 3208

NEWLYN GALLERY
Nr Penzance, Cornwall

NOTHING
The Covered Market, Oxford
tel: 0865 47084

NORTH WEST ARTS
ASSOCIATION CENTRE
52 King Street, Manchester
tel: 061 833 9471

NORTHERN ARTISTS
Leeds

NORWICH CASTLE MUSEUM
CRAFTSHOP
Norwich
tel: 0603 22233

OLD KEMBLE GALLERIES
29 Church Street, Hereford
tel: 0432 66049

ORIAN GALLERY
Penzance, Cornwall

OXFORD GALLERY
23 High Street, Oxford
tel: 0865 42731

PARK SQUARE
57 St Paul's Street, Leeds
tel: 0532 26421

PARROTS LTD
Leicester, Leicestershire

PAYNE & SON
High Street, Oxford

PETER DINGLEY GALLERY
16 Meer Street, Stratford on
Avon, Warwickshire
tel: 0789 5001

PETITTE GALLERY
Lutterworth, Leicestershire

PLEGA
Royal Mile, Edinburgh

POTIPHER
Tonbridge, Kent

POTTENBAKKER
Antwerp, Belgium

PRIMAVERA
10 King's Parade, Cambridge
tel: 0223 57708

QUADRANGLE
1 Walton Crescent, Oxford
tel: 0865 57035

RALPH LEWIS
Brighton, Sussex

ROBERT KELLY
Liverpool

ROMANIS
Chester, Cheshire

SACKVILLE GALLERY
9 Middle Row, East Grinstead,
Sussex
tel: 0342 27651

SAKS
New York, USA

SALCOMBE ART CLUB GALLERY
Salcombe, Devon

SALIX
57 Thames Street, Windsor,
Berkshire
tel: 95 62218

SAMIAN GALLERIES
Torquay, Devon

SCOPAS
16 Hart Street, Henley on
Thames, Oxfordshire
tel: 049 12 5157

SCOTTISH CRAFT CENTRE
140 Canongate, Edinburgh
tel: 031 556 8136

SEASONS
Forest Row, Sussex

SERENDIB
15 Market Place, Woburn,
Bedfordshire
tel: 052 525 464

SERGE GUILLOUX
Paris, France

SEVEN SPRINGS GALLERY
Ashwell, Hertfordshire

SPANISH GUITAR CENTRE
Bristol, Avon

STANBROOK ABBEY SALES SHOP
Callow End, Hereford &
Worcester

STUDIO 10½
Hull, Humberside

SUMAS
Windsor, Berkshire

TARRATT
Leicester

THINGS WELSH
Cardiff, South Glamorgan

THREEHOUSEHOLDS GALLERY
Threehouseholds, Chalfont St
Giles, Buckinghamshire
tel: 024 07 3010

TOWN MILLS CRAFT CENTRE
Chudleigh, South Devon

TROIKA
61 Fore Street, St Ives, Cornwall
tel: 073670 5556

WAREHOUSE
Ripon, Yorkshire

WHYMSIES
Rotherfield, Nr Crowborough,
Sussex

YEW TREE COTTAGE GALLERY
Ingleby, Stanton-on-Bridge,
Derbyshire
tel: 03116 2894